To Allison + sons

With loads of love

Sylvia

Christmas 2018

Some Book of Mormon Sonnets –

Verse by Verse

by
Tom Matkin

My Complaint

Sometimes... I beg,
"Don't try to tell me everything
in every phrase," but it's like
a hologram
every fraction contains
all the information of the whole
and who am I to
ask God to take it easy.

After all,
He wrote the book and
dared me to receive it
promising that if I would
He would give me more.
The truth of all things.
It's in the book.

The Title Page

There may be faults within this curious book
For men were used to tool its ancient script
But they obediently undertook
And so from out the dust it now has slipped.

And God has placed His witness in its leaves
To remnants of His children of each sort
A promise, to each person that receives
Of spotlessness in His Son's judgment court.

Who sets himself against this book is sure
To face that judgment overly adorned
A consequence, both terrible and poor,
A needless curse, for all are fully warned.

This record's raised to show, convince and save
Condemning it's more foolishness than brave.

The Three Witnesses

"And it is marv'lous in our eyes." They said
And in their ears the voice of God commands
Imprinting witness, fully, heart and head
With what the angel put into their hands.

To hear, to see, to feel, to understand
To know, to testify this work is true
To bear, to hold, to swear, to share, to stand
As chosen witnesses of this renew.

Oh Cowdery, Whitmer, Harris! All these three
To witness works of wonder and record
Their faithful testimonies, firm and free
The keystone to the gospel, now restored.

Each lived a troubled life, yet, to the last
Each held this testimony firm and fast.

The Eight Witnesses

No angel was enlisted to engage
These witnesses in lessons or debates
Four Whitmers and three Smiths and just one
Page
Could only see and handle Joseph's plates.

Then give a humble record of their sense
That these were works of curious ancient art
Thus junior to the witness and defense
The Three were offered as their greater part.

And yet, suppose these Eight had truly known
The things the Three were blessed to see and
hear
Would all these things be any better shown
To those who doubt, dismiss, or mock, or fear?

We have of witnesses, enough, and more
To be without excuse if we ignore.

The Testimony of Joseph Smith

It's grown from just this one to millions now
Who testify of grove in solemn voice
This youth who would not flinch nor disavow
Who said a faithful prayer for wisdom's choice.

And then, on further prayer, an angel came
In robes exceeding white and person so
Above in glory any earthly claim
To resurrect this book from long ago.

And Joseph did declare the book was true
Delivered by the gift of God to man
From golden plates to prophet. Now to you!
The fullness of salvation's gospel plan.

Beware of taking lightly Joseph's name
This angel knew it well the day he came.

A Brief Explanation about the Book of Mormon

You've got your metal plates, at least four kind
To give a sacred record of these folks.
The Plates of Nephi, small and large, remind
Of things most sacred, not of wars or jokes.

Next, Plates of Mormon, summaries I guess
With commentaries, prophesies, and notes
The sort of stuff to edify and bless
A lot of special sermons. Great for quotes!

And then the Plates of Ether are explained
This record of the Jaredites and such
With comments by Moroni, who ingrained
A lot of gospel knowledge in his touch.

Then finally, the Plates made out of Brass
The hist'ry of mankind, from first to last.

Names and Order of Books in The Book of Mormon

First Book of Nephi: Obedience is shown
The Second Book of Nephi: Wilderness
The Book of Jacob: Olive trees are grown
The Book of Enos: Mighty prayer to bless

And two too small are Jarom and Omni
The Words of Mormon sets the record straight
Mosiah features Benjamin on high
And Alma: sermons, wars and great debate.

In Helaman, more wars and politics
Third Nephi tells of Christ at Bountiful
Fourth Nephi shows, at last, a happy mix
Next Mormon calls to Christ each doubting soul.

And Ether tells of towers and of faith
Moroni tops it all, with promised grace.

1 Nephi Chapter 1

Young Nephi may have thought his parents
good
And felt his prophet father was the best
And grateful he was that he understood
The mysteries of God above the rest.

But learning what the future had to bring
And trying to be true to such a trust
Proved not to be an easy or kind thing
When found among Jerusalem's unjust.

So if you feel to pray with all your heart
To bless the future of your brethren dear
Know that while this may bring the better part
It could evoke their jealousy and fear.

It's terrible to have to say: Wo! Wo!
To most the friends and family you know!

1 Nephi 1:1

He starts by mentioning his folks and that
They taught him lots of things he valued well
It's clear this record won't be idle chat
His dealings with is family he'll tell.

He writes he's had afflictions, quite a lot,
And these we guess he'll chronicle as well
The lessons that his many troubles taught
We're sure to find he's also going to tell

And most intriguing, things of God and such!
He claims to know the mysteries quite well
And so it's promised that this book will touch
Upon the things that only God can tell.

This Nephi. Brother, son, and prophet true
Makes record! Now the rest is up to you.

1 Nephi 1:2

An upstate farm-boy writes a curious book
So full of things about which he can't know
He'll catch himself on almost every hook
His fantasy will be an ease to show.

You take this Egypt language stuff he spouts
He could not even guess how that's compiled
(His English writing aptitude leaves doubts)
So tales of ancient languages seem wild.

And how much of the Jews can someone know
Who grows up on a homestead clearing trees?
He hardly had the chance to even go
To grammar school to learn his abc's.

So reader, watch to see how Joseph meets
His claim to Ancient Near Eastern conceits.

1 Nephi 1:3

In history the source is everything
We look for primary not hearsay stuff
The witness who was there can always bring
Authority an absent can't rebuff.

Ah shoot! What made me say such rot?
The arm chair Monday morning second sorts
Are quick to analyze and declare naught
To cast great doubt on any first reports.

And so, although this writer now presents
That what he saw is true and he was there
We've learned to disbelieve such evidence
And set aside what any man may swear.

But one day I expect to meet Nephi
And look this prophet squarely in the eye.

1 Nephi 1:4

Imagine as a flock of prophet types
Descended on that quiet little town
And caused a stir with all their weighty gripes
Of how the moral conduct had turned *down*.

And picture as this band of doomsday seers
Expounded that repentance was required
And scorched unwilling hardened Judah's ears
With threats of ruin said to be inspired.

The civil unrest must have been profound
And politics a dangerous game to play
And with the monarch, now so freshly crowned
A kingdom marched towards its final day.

"WHY ME?" King Zedekiah must have cried
Each time he learned of what was prophesied.

1 Nephi 1:5

I wonder sometimes if we really draw
Our hearts out to our people like we should
Or do we rather live within a law
Which sets a dismal limit to our good.

Some agonize and worry, fiercely so!
About their people, 'specially those who stray
They fret, they fuss, the fume, they undergo,
And doubtfully, quite faithlessly, they pray.

But this suggests that faith and action could
As we go forth, increase the force of prayers
And raise the limit to imploring good
And answer all our people centered cares.

Still Lehi's faith was surely great, not small
And yet his blessing wouldn't please them all.

1 Nephi 1:6

Pillars of cloud by day and fire by night
Led captive Israel out of Egypt's clutch
And Moses surely saw things by that light
And heard until he quaked and trembled much.

And a pillar of fire on a rock
In answer came to Lehi's fervent prayer
And he too saw the light, and heard the talk
And he did quake and tremble in its glare.

And in a quiet grove a pillar came
To overcome a farm boy in his prayer
The voice, the light, the message, all the same
He quaked and trembled, changed forever there.

Each one of us will quake and tremble too
When judgment brings that pillar to our view.

1 Nephi 1: 7

Get ready for a lot of stuff like this
Exhausted people - overcome - passed out
Dog tired after rev'latory bliss
Such things are what this book is all about.

Old Lehi, Alma, Kings and Queens and more
We'll read about, would see, then call - time out!
To hit the deck to struggle to restore
What's needed by those newly made devout.

And lest you think this just an Eastern thing
An affectation of an ancient sort,
That nothing modern would such faintings bring
I pose this question of a like report.

Think, when Moroni taught from dusk to dawn
What happened to young Joseph later on?

1 Nephi 1:8

Imagine such a meeting in the sky
A time for angel officers to preach
And in the foremost seat presiding high
The First and Last. The Master. Waits to teach

A hymn to start the gathering in style
The angels in their concourses sing out
And nervously back from a nosebleed aisle
Our mortal visitor looks all about.

What luck to be invited to this scene
What joy to see this everlasting plan
What privilege to be where things unseen
Will unfold to affect the course of man.

Imagine Gen'ral Conf'rence in the sky!
As seen through Father Lehi's mortal eye.

1 Nephi 1:9

It took until the 9th verse of this book
Before the One's descent is here described
The One whose coming surely made it look
As if to Him the sun should be ascribed.

That noon day sun! That brightest thing we know
That fiery orb that warms far distant parts
That fiercest furnace, strongest potent glow
The symbol of the One who owns our hearts.

It came to pass that He came down just then
And then again and then again and more
To teach, to bless, to testify to men
To purify with fire evermore.

And countless verses after this record
Their testament of Jesus Christ our Lord.

1 Nephi 1: 10

We pass our lives, a goodly share, at night,
And should be glad for every kindly spark
When moon and stars afford the only light
To guard and shelter us against the dark.

His stars go with him almost everywhere
Each trailing bits of glory, testing men,
To see if they'll detect, although more spare
The self same light the sun gives forth again.

Some even curse the sun and disallow
The beauty and the brightness of the day
And so it's not surprising to learn how
The stars get overlooked this careless way.

And so as sure as stars will follow sun
At night, we look to them to find the One.

1 Nephi 1:11

Suppose the Lord was standing in your path
And rather than to speak, he took a book
And bade you read of great impending wrath
How strange, he scarcely spoke, just made you
look.

And what if in the book you noticed then
That it was scripture of the common kind
From Revelation or Isaiah's pen
Not something new, but something to remind.

A visit from the Lord of Hosts indeed
A chance to learn of things unknown you hope
And all He does is ask you to reread
Some things that long were well within your
scope.

So when we give the Book sufficient heed
We pretty much learn everything we need.

1 Nephi 1:12

The angels sang and heav'nly throngs adored
And Lehi humbly heard and saw it all
And bowing down before his mighty Lord
He modestly received prophetic call.

Think! Standing in a conference so grand
Amid the sounds of praises to the King
He saw before him; Oh so close at hand
The One and only Son that hope can bring.

Imagine how it must have felt to see
This grand and high majestic scene of bliss
The Sun and Stars revealed to new degree
Could anything exceed a scene like this!

And yet, when all was done and sung and said
The Spirit only filled him when he read.

1 Nephi 1:13

The Book of Mormon text is new just yet
In thirteenth verse of Nephi's book that's one
But certain themes, already now are set
A richly woven pattern has begun.

Three players on this written stage will toil:
The God of Israel, heart and soul of love,
The Devil, bent to devastate and spoil,
And Man, enticed from under and above.

And woes will be pronounced more oft than
naught
Those woes from God when righteousness
departs
When in abominations men are caught,
And carried captive by their hardened hearts.

Wo, wo, Jeruasalem! You've sealed your fate.
And now the consequence of sins await.

1 Nephi 1:14

To Thee, O Lord Almighty God! I turn
My heart, my soul, my mind, my life is thine
Tis for thy throne and mercy that I yearn
O that thy goodness would be counted mine.

And wide the reaches of thy mercy Lord
How well that thou dost shelter me and bless
And I that know thee have indeed adored
Thy works so great and fully marvelous.

Unworthy am I of thy staying hands
Yet joyful of thy power and thus sure
That none will ever perish if he stands
As witness of thy covenants secure.

Assured that thou wilt ever turn to me
O Lord Almighty God I turn to thee.

1 Nephi 1:15

I have two sons who honor me and share
Peculiarities of speech and tongue
Although the one boy still has lots of hair
It's clear he'll only have it while he's young.

A father should leave more than this behind
Much more than balding, or a spreading girth
There ought to be some traits that will remind
His progeny of higher things than earth.

Old Lehi left his sons a record of
His praises of the God of heaven high
Rejoicing at the thought of what's above
Was language that he hoped his sons might try.

I hope that what I've said and done reruns
As praises in the language of my sons.

1 Nephi 1:16

He wrote them down, those many things he saw
He wrote them down, his visions and his dreams
He wrote them down, the things that gave him
awe
He wrote them down, his sermons and his
themes.

And just because he wrote them down we know
A bit of what he saw and heard aright
Those prophesies of so so long ago
Preserved because he took the time to write.

Our prophet Spencer was a writer too
And promised angels might our words recite
And generations love our journals true
But first of all, of course, we have to write!

What's worse, to live an empty life and share
Or, live it well, yet leave the record bare?

1 Nephi 1:17

I want to tell you what I have to say
My story burns within to get without
But first I have to summarize the way
My father took this family down south.

I've scratched it out on metal plates I made
Abridged, a bit, (well, quite a bit) I guess
But still a story of a bold crusade
Against a group determined to transgress.

It may seem strange that it was I who wrote
I'm just my father's middle child, you see
And though my brothers I will sometimes quote
The bulk of what you'll hear will come from me.

Read carefully this story of my life
And learn the lasting ways of family strife.

1 Nephi 1:18

It's nice to have the Lord come visit you
And teach you what you need to know for sure
To show you what the future's going to do
And take you on a panoramic tour.

But when you realize the future's bad
For neighours, friends and people all around
It tends to make you miserable and sad...
Unless you have the chance to warn the town.

So Lehi must have been delighted when
The Lord commanded that he spill the beans
And tell before the trouble could begin
Of up and coming desolation scenes.

So off he went as cheerful as a clam
To tell his neighbours they were in a jam.

1 Nephi 1:19

Lehi had seen and heard and read their fate
And knew they must be warned, but would not heed
Abominations marked their wicked state
Destruction loomed with devastating speed.

When he explained how wickedness can kill
These people mocked! Because it made them mad.
I doubt that many even heard the drill
Describing how redemption could be had

It's funny how the truth can raise such spite
In those who think their wicked ways are fine
If they were so convinced that they were right
You'd think they wouldn't really pay much mind.

A chastening, if true, though kind in tone
Will always cut the guilty to the bone.

1 Nephi 1:20

The shouts of "Kill him!" by an angry throng
Are types and shadows of a perfect time
When perfect right confounded perfect wrong
And perfect shame turned perfectly sublime.

All history is balanced on this point
Of cataclysmic infinite recourse
A sacrifice that cannot disappoint
Delivered without limit or remorse.

And often well before and ever since
These wretched mobs of evil doers meet
To reenact the murder of the Prince
And seal their endless mis'ry with deceit.

At Carthage or at Calvary or Rome
Great prophet martyrs forge our passage home.

1 Nephi Chapter 2

I thought this family meeting would be nice
To tell you what I've had a dream about
And since I won't be asking your advice
I hope you'll hear with faith and not with doubt.

It's kinda funny what we have to do
You'll laugh, I'm sure. It caught me by surprise.
We have to bid Jerusalem adieu!
And only take the fewest of supplies.

We'll leave behind our silver and our gold
And go into the wilderness alone
That's right, my sons, it does sound kinda bold
But no. This trip we really can't postpone.

We have to go to save our lives, it seems.
Who wants to give a prayer of thanks for
dreams?

1 Nephi 2: 1

You're blessed as any in these promised lands
And faithful in the sacred things you do
Declaring to this people my commands
And by the way, they'll try to murder you.

These dreams are pretty special as you know
They set you up as having work to do
You'll have to teach these people. Oh, just so!
And by the way, they'll try to murder you.

How many prophets over all the years
Have heard the charge to teach the gospel true
And learned that when you try to save your
peers
It often seems, they'll try to murder you.

Be careful of those evil and untrue
'Cause by the way, they'll try to murder you.

1 Nephi 2:2

The wilderness may beckon some of you
A temptress calling for your heart and soul
Perhaps you cherish bathing in a slough
Or sleeping with a gopher in a hole?

The wilderness may lure you with its charms
Attracting you to it like bees to flowers
Perhaps you like the snow up to your arms
Or play out in the rain for hours and hours?

The wilderness may be to you a balm
To heal you from the pressures of your day
Perhaps to find your milk you climb a palm
And call some grubs and berries a buffet?

But as for me I find the wild dumb
Although, I guess, it beats destruction some.

1 Nephi 2:3

Some people like to fuel their fires with doubt
They test and strain at every word or sigh
They seem to have a driving need to flout
They never think to answer "yes", just "why".

The writ is full of words of faith and love
It pleads for us to be believing too
To find our earthly guidance from above
To not just yield to what we want to do.

It was because he was obedient!
A state of being, gave Lehi the power
To not succumb to the expedient
And find the Lord's directions sweet not sour.

Bless those who sing *How Gentle God's
Commands*
True saints, obedient to His demands.

1 Nephi 2:4

He packed his tent and children in the van
And left his house, and gold and silver too
Of course, he had to leave his family lands
And every precious thing they ever knew.

They took along provisions for the ride
Their years supply of dates and seeds and stuff
The sort of food that's canned or been freeze
dried
And if you eat a bit, well... that's enough.

I kind of think his wife and older boys
Were looking back as they pulled out of town
The thought of all the gems and cash and toys
They left behind was bound to get them down.

I wonder if I was in Lehi's clan
Would I be happy with this caravan?

1 Nephi 2:5

The weather on the Red Sea is quite nice
Although the summer's hot and awfully dry
There's never any snow or sleet or ice
You seldom find a cloud up in the sky.

There's lots of things to do along the beach
With golf and scuba junkets for your fun
And lay out in the sun to tan. or bleach
Then dine and hit the hot tub when you're done.

There's still some wilderness along this route
Between the tennis courts and quaint sea ports
And never noise like Cairo or Beirut
Just peaceful little holiday resorts.

And just imagine that the tall palm trees
Along this Sea, once sheltered refugees.

1 Nephi 2:6

Just think how much this simple verse betrays
In thirty words a child can understand
We find a purely Aramaic phrase
And talk that maps a trackless foreign land.

In New York every river's water-filled
And no one calls their rivers wet or dry
Yet in the desert native tongues are thrilled
To tell when water does a stream supply.

And think if you were making up a tale
About a place you could not know about
Geography in any real detail
Would trip you up as quick as you could shout.

This verse alone is footprint in the sand
To show the book came not from Joseph's hand.

1 Nephi 2:7

First build an altar, make it firm and strong
Use stones, foundation stones, not sand or straw
Then make your offering, but don't be wrong
Exactness in your sacrifice is law.

And while each rock is being understood
And offerings devised with care and love
Lift up your arms in gratitude for good
Give constant thankful praise to God above.

This verse, so plain, yet wonderful, sublime
The formula for getting through this night
Three simple steps to guide us in this time
Of proving that we're made of stuff that's right.

Could any words be found to match these few?
Exquisite recipe for what to do.

1 Nephi 2:8

In Aqaba today the beach is clean
The para sailers swoop up in the sky
The jet skis add their noise to the scene
And sunbathers, in careless clusters, lie.

The tourists visit excavation sites
Where ancient ruins poke from out the dust
And now and then an artifact excites
A sort of archeologistic lust.

And such will wonder how it was, this place
So long before the jet ski or Club Med
Who passed along this beach without a trace
Beside this coral reef and sea of Red?

Close by, an ancient river in a vale
Holds tight its secret witness of this tale.

1 Nephi 2:9

Two rovers creep across a far off orb
And scratch around in reddish dust for this
To see what evidence they can absorb
That water out there, did or now exists.

For without water, we believe we know
No life, as we do understand and see
Could ever be sustained or start or grow
In short, no living thing could ever be.

A hopeful father, sensing in his child
The signs of dying virtue may decree
That water in a river running wild
Is fitting namesake for what he could be.

I'd guess that anywhere that light be found
That living water also may abound.

1 Nephi 2:10

For symbols of embodiment of might
The peak is where the western thinking leans.
It seems we tend to look to mountain height
Not valleys, rivers or more lowly scenes.

Steadfast, immoveable and ever firm
These mountain adjectives misunderstood
The tendency of Lehi to confirm
That rivers better demonstrate what's good.

Of course the ancient eastern mind was true
Pure symbols of the best a son could be
These things are what the river valley's do
The ones that fill the fountains of the sea.

But whether mounts or valleys describe best
It seems that Lemuel failed to pass the test.

1 Nephi 2:11

It's bad enough to perish in the wild
And lose your lands and other precious things
But it would get most anybody riled
If it was due to vain imaginings.

This visionary part is what we hear
As being more than they could ever bear
"No fun" they said, to have a living seer
Directing every when, and what and where.

It sounds like Laman and his brother Lem
Would not have murmured for an instant if
These difficulties that befell to them
Had been for other reasons than this.

Much harder then, than now, to comprehend
That foolishness begins when visions end.

1 Nephi 2:12

Oh yes the constant murmuring begins
Conceited sons, so frequently distraught
Who justified their oh so many sins
Because they were the eldest of the lot.

We know they didn't know the gospel well
And what they learned they instantly forgot
Their watchword, just two syllables: "rebel"
Because they were the eldest of the lot.

Is there a bit of sympathy for them
For not receiving what should be their ought
A sense that they were cheated, Lam and Lem,
Because they were the eldest of the lot?

I'd guess their shorts are still tied in a knot
Because they were the eldest of the lot.

1 Nephi 2:13

We cannot always reconcile the two
The word of God with what the people think
To men, Jerusalem looked safe and true
God's prophet warned "This city's on the brink!"

Likewise with many things we see today
Our experts like to prophesy some too
And guesses about what was once the way
Take on a sort of quasi gospel view.

It seems okay for prophets to diverge
And those of men to scoff at what God's say
But why this animosity and urge
To seek to take God's prophet's life away?

Remember safe Jerusalem, my friend
If you prefer the prophesies of men.

1 Nephi 2:14

God's work, we think, is mostly made
By volunteers with soft and willing hearts
But when the Spirit's power is displayed
Oft times base conscripts even play their parts.

And so commands are sometimes thus obeyed
By those whose hearts are hardened among men
Though after this brief peace with God is made
They're back to disobedience again.

This notion gives me personal concern;
I wish to never be the kind that shakes
And trembles before God before I learn
To let go of my confounding mistakes.

I hope to be the sort of volunteer
Who learns to do his bit from love, not fear.

1 Nephi 2:15

A castle for an earthly king seems right
A cottage for a peasant is the norm
A president should have a house that's white
And college kids live gladly in a dorm.

Log cabins seem to suit the pioneer
And lodges serve for hunters and the like
A fort protects a soldier and his gear
A clubhouse for an angel and his bike.

A caveman, well you guess it, has his cave
And trailer trash reside inside a park
A prison is the best place for a knave
A sailor likes a houseboat or an ark.

But lowliest of all to own or rent
Would be dwell in nothing but a tent.

1 Nephi 2: 16

Exceeding young! A boy, though growing fast
Now that's the time for sober thought to start
Don't put it off until the bitter last
The youth does best who softens up his heart.

Have great desires! Not trivial demands
Upon no less than mysteries obsess
The nickel thinker never understands
The priceless ways that Godliness can bless.

Cry unto God! There's no where else to go
He'll visit you, and though you yet be young
His saving grace can bless and teach and show
You how to bend your will to father's tongue.

Profound! The patterns that this verse displays
Of consequences for the boy who prays.

1 Nephi 2:17

No blessing could be kinder or more large
To youthful Nephi, destined to preside
Who, as he met the Spirit's awesome charge
Had Sam, his faithful brother at his side.

What leader doesn't need a Sam or two
A peaceful stalwart member of the fold.
A loyal brother, friend and comrade true
The sort who just believes the things he's told.

The Aarons, Hyrums, Jonathans and such
Who second someone greater, called to lead
Who demonstrate the too uncommon touch
Of able hearts that willingly concede.

We hear too much of nay sayer and knave
God Bless this Sam! Devoted, true and brave.

1 Nephi 2 :18 and 1 Nephi 3:29

How does this work, this softening of hearts?
You pray, you plead, you preach, you teach, beseech,
And cry to God against the fiery darts
That keep the softening beyond your reach.

This agency, so frustrating and strong
The gift that every man and woman claims
The right to choose between the right and wrong
Exasperates our best intended aims.

While some abuse their privilege and try
To force a hardened heart and thus dispel
The gifts of godlike distance that apply
We influence, but we cannot compel

Why do you smite your brothers with a rod?
A question Nephi never heard from God.

1 Nephi 2: 19 and 1 Nephi 16:28 and D&C 84: 33&43

Read here, before the curious ball arrived
When simple faith and lowliness of heart
And diligence in seeking God have thrived
Great blessings have for one been set apart.

Faith, diligence and heed together made
The Liahona work its magic spell
And anyone who these three prices paid
Could take whatever blessings God would tell.

Although we still have godly compass need
The Liahona's now no longer here
Yet faithfulness, with diligence and heed
Still chart for travelers a course that's clear.

Remember faith and diligence and heed
A necessary pattern to succeed.

1 Nephi 2:20

I love the sound of guarantees of wealth
Of prospering in lands of promise too
Of happiness and cheerfulness and health
And sunny skies a constant shade of blue.

I think I favor ease and pleasure rife
Without responsibility or fear
I know I'd like a long and painless life
With nothing to provoke a frown or tear.

I like my things a cut above the rest
Substandard doesn't interest me at all
Not ever second hand or second best
I want to hear my name in the first call.

Oh wait! You say prosperity's not free?
Keep what? Perhaps these blessings aren't for me.

1 Nephi 2: 21

"A Rebel gets his Recompense" might pass
Or "Laman Leads all Losers" could define
Or "Brothers Scratched from Winning Team"
shows class
While "Cut Ups Cut Off" makes a good headline.

You need to keep this "Cut Off" phrase in mind
Because it shows up every time we hear
That when we keep commands of God we find
Great blessings of prosperity and cheer.

This constant never-ending pattern taught
Two concepts linked together start to close
This Ying and Yang of Book of Mormon thought
"Commandments" or "Cut off" is how it goes.

My hope's for: "Prospered in the Promised Lands"
Not "Cut Off 'Cause He Couldn't Keep
Commands."

1 Nephi 2:22

Some like to be the ruler and the king
To teach, to lead to be the head of state
To be top dog and wear the sovereign's ring
And be extolled as wonderful and great.

Some like to boss their elder brothers too
To rule the family roost with heavy hand
Be admiral and captain of the crew
The issuer, not subject to command.

But Nephi was submissive, meek and mild
Not dreaming of an empire or a realm
Respectful and obedient this child
A kind reluctant hand upon the helm.

I half suspect this forecast made him fret.
Was this a favored promise… or a threat?

1 Nephi 2:23

My friends I think it's time we did discuss
The way the Book of Mormon prophets wrote
How they would frame their thoughts in chiasmus
That ancient Aramaic form of note.

How they would start a sermon or a charge
Then build until they crossed that final shelf
That heart and core, the core and heart enlarge
The X point, where the thesis crossed itself.

And even in this simple homily
That form the Hebrews and their kin devised
A true chiasmus, not anomaly
These prophets understood and surely prized.

Yes friends, we need to read with this in mind
And share the holy patterns that we find.

1 Nephi 2:24

Oh my! The price we pay when we forget
This heavy, heavy, price. A scourge
To stir us up. Remind by solemn threat
Of foes that disregard will make emerge.

The very rebels play into His hand
Unwitting servants to the One they hate
The agents in a play so caref'lly planned
That no one really keeps the players straight.

What's worse? To be the scourge or be
scourgee?
To be reminded or rebel and so remind
What irony to those who disagree
That this agrees with what's in heaven's mind.

I think I'll tie my finger with a string
And hope that's 'nuff to ways of mem'ry bring.

1 Nephi Chapter 3

Ya say yer fam'ly doesn't git along!
The kids er squabblin' almost all the time
And whinin' seems to be ther fav'rite song
And some seem destined fer a life of crime.
And would it take an angel t' make peace
Between the brothers in yer humble nest
And will these difficulties never cease
And do you guess you've failed the 'parent' test.
Now take a look at father Lehi's clan
This prophet, dreamer, patriarchal guy
And know that ever since this world began
Some fam'lies never could see eye to eye.

And even God the Father lost a third
Or all that started in his pre-earth herd.

1 Nephi 15:1 and 1 Nephi 3:1

Suppose the Spirit carried you away
And showed you things you couldn't hardly tell
And showered you with wisdom's perfect ray
And put you under heaven's faultless spell.

Suppose that even questions never posed
Were answered by the Spirit as you dreamed
And nothing to your heart was undisclosed
And nothing sacred to you unredeemed.

And then, when all this spiritual affair
Had passed, and life was "everyday" again
Where would you go, the first of all, to share
To testify, to marvel, to explain?

It seems, when youthful prophet's dreams are spent
You'll find them straightway back in father's tent.

1 Nephi 3:2

Some try to figure every option well
And calculate what outcomes might be made
They take the choice to buy or hold or sell
Without regard to who suggests the trade.

For some, it doesn't matter what the tasks
They could be easy, dangerous or long
It isn't what it is, but who that asks
That brings a nasty cry of "This is wrong!"

Yet others also seem to pay no mind
To what they're asked to do, or say, or be
Their greatest care is that they clearly find
They're in accord when faced with God's decree.

To turn from Salem or return or not
These choices bother brothers quite a lot.

1 Nephi 3:3

A madman has the records of the Jews!
A thief, a cheat, a drunken bon vivante
A bully, more the master of the snooze
Than work or things of use. The dilettante!

A loser has the records of the Jews!
A trickster, crook and greedy low down slob
The sort of friend that honest folks don't choose
The master of the con and inside job.

This villain has the record of the Jews!
So proud, depraved, and totally unjust
Unworthy of the honor, he'll abuse
The privilege of such a sacred trust.

And though he's now self righteous, standing tall
The time will come when Laban's head will fall.

1 Nephi 3:4

If it's a longish trip or just a jaunt
The packing part demands your faith and heed
They say to take but half the clothes you want
And twice the money that you thought you'd
need.

And since you'll have to carry all that load
And stairs or hills or even mountain height
May stand between you and your fresh abode
It's always good advice to travel light.

But when you know your trip is pure "one-way"
And into wilderness where money's naught
For what to take you probably ought to pray
And give each choice some extra care and
thought.

One thing that seemed to come as a command
Is "Bring the scriptures to the promised land".

1 Nephi 3:5

Some Pollyanna's never cast a doubt
To them the glass is half full to the brim
They cheer and bless and raise a joyful shout
And beam and grin and smile at every whim.

While others love to weave a strong complaint
To gripe and grouse and grumble night and day
And test the patience of the bravest saint
Bemoaning and protesting all the way.

If I were bearing dangerous bad news
An errand from the Lord that made me frown
I know which ones of these I'd probably choose
To tell to get their tails hard out of town.

But Lehi's love and was probably too firm
To joy at all in watching Laman squirm.

1 Nephi 3:6

I have a friend like that, who never gripes
Profound obedience is ingrained deep
His knee jerk happiness is legend like
I'm sure he's even cheerful in his sleep.

My happy friend knows nothing of complaint
His countenance is ever clear and bright
He's quite the study of a perfect saint
And is the very essence of polite.

I used to say, "He's far too heavenly,
To be of any actual earthly good."
And smile a bit at such an irony
Well knowing it was he who understood.

The Lord may love us all, but one thing's plain
His favor follows those who don't complain.

1 Nephi 3:7

We speak of testimony from the start
Expressions of belief are shared in love
And simple faith from deep within the heart
Is poured out like the sunshine from above.

And then when pure belief is on display
I ask a simple question with a smile
"Will you accept a call?" is all I say
And quick there comes the answer without guile.

So many Nephis in the church today!
Who never think to murmur or protest
Who think of nothing else but to obey.
And answer "Yes!" before they hear the test.

I hope that I'm the sort, when called, who stands
And goes and does whatever God commands.

1 Nephi 3:8 and 3 John 1:4

There's something hardwired into us I note
That makes us want to make somebody glad
And not just anybody gets that vote
The one we like to please is good old dad.

And nothing makes a papa quite so thrilled
As hearing that his children walk in truth
Somehow that makes a daddy feel fulfilled
And gives him hope his kids might live through youth.

But if one finds he can't fill pa with joy
And sometimes feels neglected or abused
His actions then get fashioned to annoy
And everybody's happiness gets bruised.

There really isn't any neutral ground
Whenever dads and kids and pride abound.

1 Nephi 3:9

Some make a lot of going "up", not "down",
Or even going "over" to their land
But I suppose when hauling tents around
It always seems like uphill in the sand.

Yet Joseph Smith would not have had a clue
Which place was in the hills or in the vale
And so from words like these one might construe
That Nephi was the author of this tale.

And though the book is riddled with these hints
Conceits embedded in the text throughout
The Spirit only can, in fact, convince
And overcome the natural force of doubt.

But once the still small voice's work is done
We look for proofs like this one just for fun.

1 Nephi 3:10

Sometimes we craft a plan for months or years
And worry every detail like a cat
Amending, adding, fixing, changing gears
Until we've thought of every "this or that?"

The sorts of plans that must have made the Sphinx
Or China's Wall or cures for colds with cough
Where everything that anybody thinks
Has been well measured. chosen or cast off

But other times we make our plans in haste
A brain storm on the brink of action's need
Without a single moment's pause or waste
We have to pick our tactics for the deed.

But quick or slow a plan may go awry
And then the consultation turns to "why?"

1 Nephi 3:11

I've read that stuff about how casting lots
In ancient days was thought to be a way
To find the will of God, not play the slots,
Like how we think it's gambling in our day.

I'm not convinced that Nephi was so slow
To think that God would speak by drawing straws
He'd had experience with how to know
The will of God according to His laws.

But maybe it was more than simple fate
That sent brave Laman as the first to try
And win the plates by casual debate
A doubtful tact upon which to rely.

I'd guess that Nephi knew right from the start
That only faith would soften Laban's heart.

1 Nephi 3:12

I'm sure it started out real pleasant like
With talk of how the Cubs can never win
Or if the NHL might go on strike
Or when the olive harvest might begin.

And there might have been talk of who was who
Such gossip, not a little, in this town
Where status rested upon who you knew
Or if your family name was well renown.

And when the small talk finally died it seems
Our Laman must have stated his desire
And what it must have been to hear the screams
As Laban gave expression to his fire.

It's odd to find that his psychology
Was so obsessed with genealogy.

1 Nephi 3:13

How irritating to despotic types
It is when challenge to their power comes
They answer it with broad and brutal swipes
To quell the beat of any rebel drums.

A casual question even may inflame
The guilty tyrant's anxious fearful mind
And thus evoke a tirade filled with blame
Against a harmless minion thus maligned.

I'm sure what Laman thought, we've often heard:
"I only asked a simple little thing
He didn't have to get so mad. My word!
It's sure not hard to make that man's bell ring!"

This lesson then is easy to recite:
"Oppressors can't say "no" and be polite."

1 Nephi 3:14

You have a plan, it's mighty good, you think
But something goes awry and wrecks your deal
And in a flash you're on the very brink
Of giving up and turning on your heel.

How many prizes won were seeming lost
Yet with repeated tries the trophy claimed?
How many prizes lost were there to win
And some apparent bobble falsely blamed?

To know the time to quit or stay the fight
To have the luck, the wisdom and the nerve
To see the consequence and chose it right
That's more than any of us could deserve.

Still, if the errand's one of God's devise
Don't ever run back home without the prize.

1 Nephi 3:15

Sometimes we have to take an oath, of course
Resolve beyond ourselves to hold the line
At once to call upon our own resource
And marry that with force that's more divine.

A promise, pledge, a covenant, a vow,
A guarantee that we will never fall
Not for ourselves, not for our here and now
But for the God to whom we owe it all.

Such undertakings freely done give power
The added strength of resolution sure
And binds the word of God in very hour
To make eventual victory secure.

I will not go down to my father's tent
Until the thing is done for which I'm sent.

1 Nephi 3:16

They must have wondered at the time just why
They left their riches home when heading out
That gold and silver could be used to buy
A lot of what you'll need along the route.

So thinking now to use it as a bribe
To get the sacred plates they needed so
They might have felt to natur'lly ascribe
This notion to a heaven in the know.

But yet, a lesson would indeed unfold
A principle or doctrine from the Lord
That sacred gifts are never bought with gold
Although sometimes they're purchased with the sword.

We learn much more from plans that go awry
Than winning on the first and only try.

1 Nephi 3:17 (and Alma 12:9-11)

The fruits of wickedness are pretty bleak
It chains you down and makes you stupid too
And when you've rode it to its very peak
It will, in very deed, destroy you.

There is no slipping by or ducking out
No feigning or finesse will fool your fate
The consequence of sin is beyond doubt
The outcome not material for debate.

There's someone knows your destiny I fear
If you are in iniquity's embrace
Like Lehi they've the power of a seer
To know you're rooted in destruction's place.

But constant sinning earns your right to be
Unfeeling, blind and heedless to their plea.

1 Nephi 3:18

Some drift away or move along or leave
Some disappear, or travel on, or split
Some go away, make tracks, or just deceive
The people left behind to think they've quit.

Some come right back almost before they're
gone
Their promise to depart a sort of game
They say they will be lastingly withdrawn
But actually their address stays the same.

But those who really really leave the scene
Whose quitting you can take as guarantee
Are those whose exit can't be called routine
They don't just calmly go away. They flee!

It takes a lot of faith in God's commands
Before you'll gladly flee from out your lands.

1 Nephi 3:19

Some plan to leave an heritage of cash
A fortune for their children when they die
They save and scheme and worry 'bout their
stash
And fret about who should get what, and why.

Some others vow to leave some souvenir
They hoard their pictures, rings or handwork sewn
And nothing gives them more of fright or fear
Than thinking these might in the trash be thrown.

But God decrees we leave a thing more rare
A record of our doings on this earth
A genealogy to give each heir
A journal which could be of endless worth.

If you leave only trinkets or some gold
Your legacy will sadly be untold.

1 Nephi 3:20

What ties us to the ancients but this writ?
These prophesies, pronouncements and decrees
These stories, psalms and proverbs loosely knit
So every willing soul is blessed by these.

What ties us to the heavens but this writ?
Delivered by the power of God above
Affirming, healing, teaching, making fit
The sinner to be saved by God's own love.

What ties us to the future but this writ?
The coming forth of lasting rays of hope
Of promise, joy, and judgment's true commit
Instruction with eternity for scope.

It's well to preserve for a promised land
The words of holy prophets by command.

1 Nephi 3:21

Why must I always be the one to plead
To nag, to teach, to tease, to try to sway
Against the odds to hope I might succeed
In turning them towards the better way?

They never seem to tire of faithlessness
Of doubt, they have... no doubt! Much less a
qualm
Their stamina for this is bottomless
Complaint their steady friend and constant
psalm.

And all I want for them is for their best
Desires that transcend what they deserve
It's not like I am on some selfish quest
I'm only bound to warn, to beg, to serve.

Persuasion's not as fun as it might seem
There's times it makes me feel like I could scream.

1 Nephi 3:22

To get our precious things and gold and such
We must go down, oh yes, we must go down
To get the trinkets that we love so much
We must go down, oh yes, we must go down.

If we would make a bribe or pay some graft
We must go down, oh yes, we must go down
A sweetener by cash or banker's draft
We must go down, oh yes, we must go down.

Unholy offering for sacred spoil
A trade that just might work, or so we thought
And hasting down we hoped no one would foil
Our plan to buy the prize we bravely sought.

Some things defy the nickel or the dime
So going down to get them wastes your time.

1 Nephi 3:23

I'm guessing Laban lived up on the bench
The high rent district in his native town
Away from common people and the stench
Of things that tend to gravitate to "down".

He would have had a view of everything
The temple and the mountains and the sky
And probably the palace of the king
Was never very far from Laban's eye.

And people, likely, coming by to see
This chief among society's elite
Would often bow on trembling bended knee
To place their gifts at mighty Laban's feet.

And even now when favors are required
You must go "up" to ask for what's desired.

1 Nephi 3: 24

Engraven on the palms of holy hands
Engraven in the hearts of contrite saints
Engraven by a finger, ten commands
The way to break from Satan's planned restraints.

Engraven in the brass of sacred plates
Engraven in the ore of promised lands
Engraven in your countenance and traits
The image of the One who understands.

All this on paper now and on the 'net
A gift as free and common as the air
But precious then and others seemed a threat
To those who held the keys to keep or share.

But though these books now cost far less than gold
Their value, when engraven, is untold.

1 Nephi 3:25

Some get addicted to the evil weed
Some others to the storied barley brew
But nothing ever ever will exceed
The troubles pride and envy can construe.

Across the fence the greener grass invites
The other guy's stuff seems to call your name
His treasure, your desire now incites
Forgotten are the rightful things you claim.

Each robbery begins with this in mind
And quite a lot of murders also do
The monster jealousy will often find
Some way to stir up violence in you.

How many sad events as history's told
Began with lust for someone else's gold?

1 Nephi 3:26

The precious things we carry day to day
The baggage and the burdens that we bear
Do oft times become needless on our way
If something fills us with an awful scare.

What's dear to us when things are going well
What's treasured most the time by anyone
Will quickly lose its ordinary spell
When chilling danger chases off all fun.

We jettison our fuel in a storm
We overboard our cargo in a gale
We drop our coat when sunshine gets too warm
We pack real light when ordered into jail.

Why do we cling so gladly to our load
When it's so quickly dumped when things
explode?

1 Nephi 3:27 (With Apologies to T.S. Eliot)

They searched the hills, they hunted far and wide
They must have called up 911 and more
And looked wherever people usually hide
But didn't ever in our cave explore.

They didn't find our cavity at all
They didn't find us holed up in a rock
I'm sure they must have thought that we might crawl
Into a cave without a door or lock.

They must have looked in all the cavities
That they could find around our holy town
Wherever monsters of depravities
Have always crept so as to not be found.

A cavity? A cavity? But where?
They searched but found our cavity. Not there!

1 Nephi 3:28

Lo livid Laman Lemuel losers lashing
Big bully brothers baby brothers beat
Conniving constant cunning countless clashing
Divided, daring, discordant defeat.

Ho! Harsh, half hearted hearkening hard hence
Pretentious posing pretenders proposed
To test, to try, to tempt, to trash, too tense
Extensive endless enmity exposed.

Yo! Yes, your youthful yearnings yielding yet
An answer aggravating and awesome
Forgotten friendless fiends forever fret
Belying beauty buds before blossom.

Since simple sibling sinfulness set seeds
So sad such sorry suffering succeeds.

1 Nephi 3:29

Sometimes the cavalry comes just in time
To save someone who's in a des'prate way
And thump the foe before he ends his crime
The storied way to make or save the day.

In scripture writings angels sometimes play
The role of cavalry when things look bleak
They pluck one prophet from his disarray
But others. well. their blood is left to speak.

I guess we'll know why some were saved or not
When everything is shown in the end
But just for now there's myst'ry in each plot
We guess why God the cavalry did send.

But one thing ought to never cause us loss
No cavalry was sent to Calvary's cross.

1 Nephi 3: 30

He didn't stick around to nag and harp
The angel didn't mince his words a bit
His questions both rhetorical and sharp
He spoke his peace and then he up and split.

It should have been enough that he was there
A lifetime of assurances and dread
Enough to make them take some extra care
Before discounting ev'rything he said.

Yet visitors can't do the soft'ning part
Not angel, demon, weasel nor great saint
Such change comes only from within the heart
Responding to the very soul's complaint.

The agency of man is firm and strong
Not bothered by a visit - short or long.

1 Nephi 3: 31

It's all about the "after" part my friend
The time when angel interventions done
When only you decide to hold or bend
And it's discovered who has really won.

We all get visits, witnesses, or such
We each are blessed sometime to know the way
It's when the visit's over that we touch
To see if faith or doubt will win the day.

It's all about remembering my friend
Remembering the angels in our lives
Some "mighty man" will constantly contend
The winner is which memory survives.

"Then why not us?" Indeed. A query true.
How quick forgetfulness wins over you.

1 Nephi Chapter 4

A household littered with these sacred books
In almost every nook or shelf like place
Ubiquitous but free from second looks
Almost unread, just occupying space.
So cheaply do we buy them here and now
That every child has sets he calls his own
And easy replication will allow
Great universal access to be shown
Still, one was once beheaded to procure
These words for chosen prophets and their kin
And by the Spirit's voice we can be sure
That what was done was free from blame or sin.

And yet, this drunkard's blood might leave a stain
On those who treat these scriptures with distain.

1 Nephi 4:1

'Tis fine to boast of all that Godly might
That built the universe and reigns above
But when we're faced with some unequal fight
Down here on earth, it gives our faith a shove.

Right in your face are foes whose pow'r is fierce
Their arms as strong as steel and thighs like trees
With evil eyes that penetrate and pierce
Quite numberless these forceful enemies!

So we must exercise a faith profound
And compensate for puffery at hand
Remembering the peace and rest that's found
Beyond these false illusions far too grand.

It takes a bit of pluck and cheer and charm
To conquer situational alarm.

1 Nephi 4: 2

Dry, dry, dry, dry, dry, dry, dry, dry, dry ground
Be strong, be strong, be strong, be strong, be strong
Armies, armies, armies, armies all drowned.
Came through, came through, came through, and not around.

Divide, divide, divide, divide, divide
Red Sea, Red Sea, it won't be set us
As hither and thither the Sea subsides
Let us go up, let us go up, let us....

Out, out, out, out, out, out, out, out, out, out
Dry dry, strong strong, up, up, free, free, free, free
The armies of Pharaoh. The armies shout
The Sea! Save me! The Sea! Save me! The Sea!

So let us be like Moses, like Moses
At least that's what this book proposes.

1 Nephi 4: 3

What Nephi says makes perfect sense of course
Who doesn't know that God is great and strong?
His brothers more than most, had felt his force
How could they time and time again go wrong?

But knowing God is strong is not the trick
The problem lies in having faith in him
Believing that he'll use that power quick
To save you against odds that look too grim.

These brothers didn't doubt what God could do
But feared he simply wouldn't help them out
How could their confidence wax strong and true
When all they ever did, with might, was pout?

Behind the doubt there's always simple sin
The faithful must be virtuous within.

1 Nephi 4: 3 (#2)

The Lord did do a number on Egypt
He plagued them quite a bit then washed them
clean
And Nephi sees this pattern as a script
For future and for scenes that might have been.

A warning of destruction for those who
Would snub the call to set His people free
And so it would not come out of the blue
When Laban's fate was settled by decree.

Foreshadowing this most conflicted choice
These words of Nephi helped prepare his way
And echoed in his heart, his very voice
Predicting Laban's death that very day.

A tender mercy, just before He'd ask
This prophet to perform this grisly task.

1 Nephi 4: 4

Sometimes we follow to the higher ground
A prophet, priest or king or president
And murmuring so as we're upward bound
It's clear we won't be long there resident.

There is a wall that's built by our complaints
That keeps us out from where the summit's sure
And leaves us, as it were, without restraint
Against our falling back to where we were.

These coat tail climbs where curiosity
Is mostly why we bother to ascend
Are marked by an escape velocity
That all our wishful thinking can't transcend.

Still, we can stop the plunge at any time
By softening our hearts against the climb.

1 Nephi 4: 5

Let's synchronize our watches if we can
And if I don't return by… six o'clock
Go back to where the family is camped
Til then, stay safely hidden in this rock.

I'll find the house of Laban in the dark
While you guys slumber in your cave of stone
Your efforts won't provide the smallest spark
Foreshadowing atonement made alone.

I will not let this mission pass me by
Its cup of trouble I will freely drink
I'll get the plates of Laban, Or I'll die!
Salvation or disaster's on the brink.

To creep into this night all on my own
A pattern every faith filled life has known.

1 Nephi 4: 6

It may appear he didn't have a plan
Not knowing every detail of the day
But truth be told before his quest began
The end was guaranteed to go his way.

"Led by the Spirit" made the outcome sure
A warranty as precious as 'tis rare
It trumps all other ways that we secure
The end result of any great affair.

The premiums for a policy like this
May seem a little steep to some of us
But those who feel the corresponding bliss
Will testify it's always worth the fuss.

You cannot buy insurance for such risks
Just qualify. And then accept the gifts.

1 Nephi 4: 7

He left the doubts of reason and of men
Behind him, back behind the city wall
Alone and in the dead of night he then
"Went forth" to answer this unlikely call.

Enough before him had also gone "forth"
To teach the pattern of God's testing ways
To ask a son or daughter to turn north
When reason pointed south for happier days.

Like Abraham or Moses or the Son
Like Gideon or Joseph or Barak
Like Samuel or Samson, everyone
Must faithfully go "forth" upon this track.

Somedays it may be just as hard for you
To sally "forth" in what you're called to do.

1 Nephi 4: 8

Here's something kind of strange, you have to think
Our Laban passed out in the street that way
The victim of affection for the drink
He chose to celebrate his lucky day.

The bounty of the wealth from Lehi's spread
Had tumbled, if you please, into his lap
And feeling heaven's smile thus on his head
He'd drunk so much he took a public nap.

And now his luck, it seems, began to change
Like robbers in the ashes of Pompeii
His fortune was short lived by the exchange
Of treachery for pleasures of the day.

And meanwhile Nephi's luck, likewise was changed
The victim and the victor rearranged.

1 Nephi 4: 9

We want to lay up treasure up above
Not down here where the rain and rust corrupt
We ought to fill our treasure chests with love
Not gold or things that earthly cares disrupt.

But sometimes something corporal and real
A thing that you can hold or even clutch
A thing that's made of matter... maybe steel
Will have significance beyond its touch.

This sword will be a thread that acts like that
A symbol that will pass from then to now
The scepter of the righteous in combat
Against the powers that hellish men avow.

Pure gold, fine work, and precious steel: this sword.
A pattern for all weapons of the Lord.

1 Nephi 4: 10

To test the very best of men, it seems
There must be more than just a righteous task
And so we find unfair excessive schemes
Bound up in what the Lord may duly ask.

Where values and a new command collide
(And anyone would shrink from such a call)
Hard lessons of obedience applied
To single out the ones who'll give their all.

These great ones have defied the reasoned ways
They shrank, then drank, the awful bitter cup
Thus qualified for high eternal praise
Their souls in heaven have been lifted up.

Yet some, from almost any task will shrink
And worse, at last, refuse to take their drink.

1 Nephi 4: 11

Sometimes there's moments frozen in our minds
Those times we can remember every thought
When something overwhelming like dark blinds
Shuts out what's all around us overwrought.

This focus of the mind at such a time
Produced in Nephi instant reasons why
The life of Laban, steeped as such in crime,
Might be demanded by the Lord on high.

Despite these worthy reasons well rehearsed
He was no executioner by right
And though he knew the man deserved the worst
His heart was still conflicted by this plight.

But still, I'm sure, it helps to understand
Whenever God puts someone in your hand.

1 Nephi 4: 12

I'm counting now and this makes three demands
And three, I think, is usually all you get
Two "Slays" and one "delivered in thy hands"
So far polite. The next might be a threat!

It's getting to decision time my friend
I know the pick of options does seem tough
But you must tell me now what you intend
Was talk of "go and do"ing just a bluff?

This is a public street now after all
And someone could be coming round the bend
With no more opportunity to stall
This drama now is coming to its end.

With only these two choices left in play.
It's deal or no deal Nephi, whaddya say?

1 Nephi 4: 13

The Lord has righteous purposes we're told
Yet sometimes someone's mischief takes a run
At interfering with what should unfold
And so the Lord must see that something's done.

And He could simply stop that wicked heart
Or hold the breath of "Labans" till they die
And who could know but what He takes that part
Against some portion of those who defy?

And yet the pattern that we see robust
Is asking someone else to do the deed
And sweep the man or nation up like dust
To clear the path for what His people need.

It's tough to be the one swept out the room
But almost just as hard to hold the broom.

1 Nephi 4: 14

Young Nephi, not yet married, still a youth
Remembered that the Lord had made a vow
To bless his seed conditional on the truth
Of how the Lord's commandments they'd allow.

And further in his thinking on this point
He recognized that trouble would arise
And likely were his seed to disappoint
Unless he won this precious brassy prize.

And every future parent ought to know
His seed will prosper just to the degree
He makes an earnest sacrifice to show
That accessing commandments is the key.

Is my example such that I'll succeed
In planting with my seed, the things they need?

1 Nephi 4: 15

Consider once again the great degree
Of change in how the law can now be heard
In CD's, DVD and MP3
Once famished, we now feast upon the word.

Like brazen serpents raised above the sick
We barely have to turn to find the law
And be saved from our illness double quick
By fixing our attention on its awe.

Still, other ensigns scream to catch our eye
And numbing doubt can yet debilitate
So many still refuse to even try
Denying that which would facilitate.

While Nephi strived to get his folks the book
Our problem is to get our bunch to look.

1 Nephi 4: 16

I wonder where these plates of brass came from
Not like the dead sea scrolls of later fame
Not parchment which would soon the dust
become
These metal leaves more permanent became.

Engraved upon them was the law, he said
But also, as we know they gave new form
A strange and wondrous golden metal thread
The practice of engraving thus was born.

And so, so far, beyond the laws in brass
An history profound in gold began
Best suited so that it would truly last
A crucial moment in God's long term plan.

A Cadillac of records was required
To meet the many needs that God desired.

1 Nephi 4: 17

This "knowing" is a "tender mercy" thing
The confluence of things at just a time
To answer some especial need, and bring
A blessing strictly personal... sublime.

Intelligence beyond his days expressed
This comprehension that coincidence
Did not play any part in how his quest
Should end in fatal fateful incidence.

Into his hands, then, such a promised gift
As conscience could now easily accept
Despite the innocence this chore would lift
No doubt, his higher call would now be kept.

Aren't "tender mercies" always just this way
Reminders of our part in heaven's play.

1 Nephi 4: 17 (#2)

When you make a solemn declaration
To go and do whatever you are asked
And when you get an explanation
Of solid reasons why this all was tasked.

When you understand the mighty power of God
And know that He is strong and on your side
And dream of holding to the iron rod
And take the scorn of brothers in your stride.

And when you qualify to see the Lord
And He sends angels to your beck and call
And teaches you the history of the world
And all about atonement and the fall.

You still might wonder why it came to be
That you were picked to slay this enemy.

1 Nephi 4: 18

So well he must have merited his fate
We only met him just the day before
And so far all he's done, without debate
Bespeaks of criminality hardcore.

I'm sure he never dreamed of such an end
The day he took delivery of his blade
How could he guess or ever apprehend
How great it was, this error he had made.

We call delicious, ironies thus laid
When rascals end up stuck by their own steel
And feel the brutes deserve to be thus paid
To die without requesting a last meal.

Still there's a wider pattern to take note
That everyone's own sword lies at his throat.

1 Nephi 4: 19

Beheading's such a messy bloody sport
It makes me wonder how he got it done?
Some do it like a baseball swinging sort
Of double handed out of park home run.

Still others, probably, more like on links
They swing from up above and scalp the ground
The divot that they take, it's what I think
Is where the victim's head would now be found.

And some might make a tennis players slash
Or like a royal polo player's swat
Or wind up and unleash to make their gash
Just like some hockey player's great slap-shot.

Without a Laundromat to clean the mess
He couldn't play this game without finesse.

1 Nephi 4: 20

Sometimes I wish I had a few more things
Those assets that return investment wealth
Some stocks and bonds and gold and even rings
To show that my portfolio's in good health.

But other times I see how this deceives
The one who has these things must keep a vault
To guard his goods against a world of thieves
And thus becomes imprisoned by default.

When we build walls to lock the world out
With bricks and iron bars and things akin
It isn't just a treasury made stout
We also tend to lock our own selves in.

My treasury is not the walk-in kind
My only treasure's in my heart and mind.

1 Nephi 4: 21

What's this about the garments and the sword
The scriptures talk about these things a lot
Can these connections safely be ignored
As just a part of this our story's plot?

The root of "garment" gives as other words
To "garnish", "garnishee" and "garner" too
Each one makes clear attachments much like
"girds"
These coverings protect from what's untrue.

A sword that's clean and pure will yield to none
Connoting sharper more combative arts
When evil must be forcefully undone
It severs, splits, divides and rends in parts.

We need clean garments, but, so says the Lord
You're never fully dressed without His sword.

1 Nephi 4: 22

One wonders. Was it some occasion grand
Or just a weekly poker rendezvous
Or business that got somehow out of hand
That caused our hero Laban to get stewed.

Or did he skip out early from the Jews
And visit other forms of friendly fare
Was all this just a story to excuse
Some sordid secret over night affair?

It doesn't really matter very much
Just how he got so drunk when he went out
His man, at least, was clearly well in touch
With what he was supposed to be about.

So often when we chit chat, between men
The truth's a hostage to what should have been.

1 Nephi 4: 23

The instances of such deceit are few
Among the chosen prophets of the Lord
But Abraham deceived, and Joseph too
As ancient scripture passages record.

And Moses likely was not quite forthright
With all he'd done and of his future plans
When he negotiated for the flight
Of captive Israel and all her clans.

And even Christ when questioned by his foes
Would sometimes give an answer quite obscure
And Nephi here, by failing to expose
Made longer life for Zoram more secure.

It's best, I think, sometimes the less you know
When knowing might just multiply your woe.

1 Nephi 4: 24

It's such a strange description of the task
To carry not the plates, but what's engraved?
It makes me ponder, wonder and to ask:
Why this rhetoric styling of what's saved?

It could be how a scratching error was
Repaired by adding phrases on the run
Or remnants of Hebraisms because
That's sometimes how translating just get done.

Or maybe Nephi understood by then
That brass or gold or leather or clay shards
Were insignificant distinctions when
The word of God was what was in the cards.

It's made me think about this greatest good:
To carry those engravings where I should.

1 Nephi 4: 25

The master's foremost call was ever so
To servants of low rank or high degree
He beckons, bids, invites, as he will go
His servant must obey, "Come follow me."

No servant ever was more greatly changed
By simple kind instructional decree
Than how this servant's life was rearranged
When Nephi simply said, "Come follow me."

It gave him freedom and an honored place
And saved him from destruction as we'll see
When Nephi looked this servant in the face
And bade him gently come, "Come follow me."

Another Master makes this guarantee
To all who heed the call "Come follow me."

1 Nephi 4: 26

What luck to by good fortune be deceived
And struck by fate and not a choice made free
To fall in league with, yet still unperceived
A prophet, priest and honored king to be.

So like what sins by consequence admit
So blind, so innocent, so unaware
Already in dilemma's deep deep pit
How could so kind a chance be so unfair?

Perhaps the real mistake lies in the view
That ever do we know of what we see
And thinking that such masquerades are true
We follow sometimes when we ought to flee.

I wonder how my providence compares
With Zoram's unintentional affairs?

1 Nephi 4: 27

How like us now to gossip of our friends
And chatter of their foibles and their fears
Dissecting by such cold infertile ends
Our underlings, superiors and peers.

While Zoram tried to play the usual game
Of back and forth with Laban's politic
I'd guess that Nephi's part was pretty lame
His thing… to get beyond that wall… and quick.

And so, it seems, so easy was deceit
Poured out on chatty Zoram as they walked
Should he have been more thoughtful and discrete
He might have noticed something as he talked.

When all you do is think of things to say
You might neglect some signs that say "Wrong Way".

1 Nephi 4: 28

He should be back by now, you'd have to think
He said to only wait 'til six o'clock
He said our watches all should be in sync
To tell us when to leave this awful rock.

Who's that that comes? Oh, worse than you could guess!
See what the early dawning light reveals
Not Nephi, but instead, in battle dress
It's Laban with his servant at his heels.

Oh woe is us. It can't be just by chance
That this demonic murderer appears
He must have caught our brother in advance
And somehow learned that we were in arrears.

And so these brothers panic, unaware
That God's already settled this affair.

1 Nephi 4: 29

Sometimes the cavalry comes just in time
To save someone who's in a des'prate way
And thump the foe before he ends his crime
The storied way to make or save the day.

In scripture writings angels sometimes play
The role of cavalry when things look bleak
They pluck one prophet from his disarray
But others. well. their blood is left to speak.

I guess we'll know why some were saved or not
When everything is shown in the end
But just for now there's myst'ry in each plot
We guess why God the cavalry did send.

But one thing ought to never cause us loss
No cavalry was sent to Calvary's cross.

1 Nephi 4: 30

A host of hints must surely have presaged
The sudden knowledge things were going wrong
And trembling now his confidence upstaged
His "fight" dissolved. His "flight" reflex grew strong.

But just that brief and tremulous delay
That moment to digest the options slim
Was all it took to guarantee his stay
And nullify his great escaping whim.

It almost looks like four things cornered him
Imposter, brothers, wilderness and wall
Surrounded, trapped, the forecast looking grim
Misfortune, he supposed, would be his call.

If suddenly the world was come undone
Who wouldn't only think to turn and run?

1 Nephi 4: 31

It's all about the "after" part my friend
The time when angel interventions done
When only you decide to hold or bend
And it's discovered who has really won.

We all get visits, witnesses, or such
We each are blessed sometime to know the way
It's when the visit's over that we touch
To see if faith or doubt will win the day.

It's all about remembering my friend
Remembering the angels in our lives
Some "mighty man" will constantly contend
The winner is which memory survives.

'Then why not us?" Indeed. A query true.
How quick forgetfulness wins over you.

1 Nephi 4: 31 (#2)

Pretend that in this struggle between men
The holder is the Lord and you've been held
It's not too great a stretch, I think, if then
You focus on the power that's used to quell.

God's Son holds each of us in His control
He bought us in the garden long ago
Wherein He paid the purchase price in full
And now He stoops to kindly let us go.

Before He does He'll give some good advice
And ask for us to promise to return
Then gently, oh so gently turn the vice
To loosen it so we can go and learn.

The metaphor is holding you and me
Let's see what happens when it sets us free.

1 Nephi 4: 32

Just like that serpent raised before the sick
Just like that water which can quell all thirst
It's real, it's not deception or a trick
He raised Himself as resurrection's first.

And so because He lives and as we live
He offers as an oath to every one
The gift that only such a God can give
With promises that cannot be undone.

See in this servant, trembling, in his hands
And in the holder, offering to save
The shadows of ourselves in earthy bands
With offerings of freedom for the slave.

So hearken and obey, and I'll save you
You can't beat that for what we need to do.

1 Nephi 4: 33

If you were wondering if this was wrong
Too much of little made into a lot.
Too much contrived, too tortured all along
Too much read into to patterns of a plot.

Well, add to this the sequence of events
That gave announcement to that holy birth
Wherein the angel heralding presents
The Savior of the heavens and this earth.

His words find echo in the struggle here
As introduction to the saving plan
He tell all earthly captives, "Not to fear"
Their Savior has arrived; the Son of man!

And read "like unto us" in Nephi's plea
Compared to Jesus Christ's: "like unto me"

1 Nephi 4: 33 (#2)

And in this sequence of events, the fall
Is patterned by the capture of the man
His freedom now depends upon the call
Of what is offered in the wondrous plan.

Out of the garden of his innocence
He stumbles into wilderness of choice
And everything he does adds consequence
To promises his captors gladly voice.

Freed by the very capture of his soul
And promised with an oath to stay that way
We hope and urge this servant to extol
And never denigrate his rescue day.

This servant newly born, what will he do?
The question which attends each man's debut.

1 Nephi 4: 34

Mark how three promises are made by now
Each one a sacred oath by God inspired
The culmination of the what and how
Success in earthly passages required.

First rescue from the certain deaths of man
Then agency, the right of freedom's way
To any who agreed to keep the plan
Is promised to the ones who will obey.

And then comes what is kindest, sweetest, best
The gift of standing, ownership... of place!
A mansion. Home. Now heavenly addressed
And blessed to be with God and see his face.

Oh happy servant, soon to be true friends
Thrice blessed when such a captor
condescends.

1 Nephi 4: 35

At first he made a promise to go down
To find a father in the wilderness
And seek his own inheritance and crown
By covenant be qualified to bless.

And then he made an oath to seal the pact
Much more than simply promising as much
This swearing was a solemn fateful act
And binding in the sight of God as such.

It seems we've lost our feeling for this sort
Of conscience binding fastening of wills
And no one hesitates to make resort
To seek to renegotiate his bills.

But God, like Zoram, never plays that trick
When he makes oaths and covenants, they stick!

1 Nephi 4: 36

If what we now call CSI was there
The Jews might have been able to detect
That Laban's death was not a murder where
The missing servant was the chief suspect.

But CSI and all its new techniques
Were not a part of legal wranglings then
And so I'm sure for weeks and weeks and weeks
He was among their ten most wanted men.

I'm guessing Zoram understood this thing
Knew what their legal systems were about
That servants of a murdered priest or king
Don't get the benefit of any doubt.

So this worked out for both equally good
To keep their flight as quiet as they could.

1 Nephi 4: 37

In jurisprudence, modern, understood
The taking of a promise by duress
Denies the need of it to be made good
It's not what we'd depend upon, I'd guess.

We're "off the hook" it seems if someone's threats
Are used to make us covenant and swear
And we can break our pledge without regrets
As soon as we escape our captor's scare.

And even worse than that a lot of folk
Get out of vows they made without a doubt
Because an independent lawyer bloke
Was not called in to tell them all about.

But scholars say that ancient oaths weren't so
I wonder how young Joseph Smith could know?

1 Nephi 4: 38

Imagine all the differences of mind
As these, our pilgrims, slogged across the sand
Aware, at times, of what was left behind
Then later thinking of some promised land.

One seeing on his sandal flecks of blood
Another thinking of an oath he'd made
Another's anger rising like a flood
While taking jealous note of Laban's blade.

The sun shone down on each about the same
The heat and wind and weather was alike
Yet as they marched together some felt blame
While others counted blessings on this hike.

And taking turns to carry those brass plates
A burden one man loves. The other hates.

1 Nephi Chapter 5

Sariah lost her cool in Chapter Five
A mother's anguished cries of deep despair
When, doubting that her sons were still alive
She told her husband that his dreams weren't fair.
And yet exceeding gladness filled her heart
As soon as all the boys were safely back
And she, it seemed, resumed the better part
Resolved to keep to strait and narrow track.
I wonder as she saw what came to pass
As hardships mounted and her family grew
If as she looked upon those plates of brass
It ever caused her sorrow to renew?

This mother of both sinners and of saints
Must always have been struggling with complaints.

1 Nephi 5: 1

The ancient promise had it right for sure
Twas to the woman God directly said
She'd have a life of sorrow… insecure
As she brought children forth… it was with dread.

The mother mourns much more than life deserves
Her fears exceed the probable results
Each possibility gets on her nerves
From birth, through childhood and as adults.

And when, defying all her greatest fears
Her children come home safely from their wars
Exceeding gladness best described by tears
Her brief relief from worry underscores.

And dads are happy too when kids come back
But "Where's the plates?" His welcoming attack.

1 Nephi 5: 2

The kind of faith it takes to be the one
Anointed to portray the holy life
Destined to live without the usual fun
Is hard to find in both the man and wife.

We hope to find our leaders in a yoke
That's equal with their partners in the house
Because we know devotion can provoke
Discord when it's resented by the spouse.

It looks like there is some of this upset
With Lehi and Sariah in their tent
She's not completely comfortable yet
With Lehi's call and visionary bent.

And when a house divides here just a crack
The kids sometimes will find the lesser track.

1 Nephi 5: 3

The language here will sadly be rehearsed
By children and grand children too for sure
And so a family's forever cursed
By murmurings that echo ever more.

Who knows but what Sariah's folks were thus
And that she learned complaining in her crib
So as she learned to talk, she learned to cuss
Like pabulum dribbled down upon her bib.

We might well take a lesson from this tale
Of intergenerational free runs
That takes a weakness down a family trail
From fathers or the mothers to the sons.

We ought to end these cycles here and now
And start new patterns that will bless somehow.

1 Nephi 5: 4

Look Sweetie, what you say is very true
I am a visionary sort of guy
And I'm sorry that it so bothers you
But it's okay and now I'll tell you why.

It's in the book, I think you will recall
That when they have no vision people will
Not only stumble, stagger, trip and fall
Not only feel despondent, sad and ill.

Not only be unlucky, underpaid
Not only have intentions go awry
Not only will they fail to make the grade
But when they lack in vision, PEOPLE DIE!

We do not want to perish do we Dear?
Be grateful I'm a visionary seer.

1 Nephi 5: 5

I hope you have observed that Lehi's mind
Was set at ease by promises to come
He didn't have to wait to seek and find
He knew where these assurances came from.

For faith is not in evidence of course
Or in observing just the usual stuff
Instead it's when we recognize the source
Then act as if that's fully quite enough.

And Lehi was so faithfully elite
That no distinction could be ever found
Between the past and what was not complete
For him twas all as one eternal round.

You have to be in awe of his belief
Yet recognize how it caused others grief.

1 Nephi 5: 6

He served up comfort to her, best he could
And she returned his serves with anxious force
Each spun the ball from where each player stood
The object was to win the match of course.

And in this serve and volley sort of game
Where players fight to reach the highest score
And someone wins and someone's left to blame
What's lost is always good *esprit de corps*.

I guess we can't know just how rough it was
Between our players on this sandy court
But this transcended routine games because
So much would later hang upon this sport.

Six – Love's a tennis score to warm your heart
But in the game of love that's not so smart.

1 Nephi 5: 7

It seems the things that Lehi said were naught
In giving comfort to the mother's fears
It wasn't till she saw the boys she sought
That she was able to suppress her tears.

Once safely in the nest with this her brood
This mother hen was comforted… content
The evidence displaced her anxious mood
And put away her motherly torment.

We sometimes see a missionary mom
Who cannot rest until her boy's return
She counts the hours and under any calm
She's always boiling over with concern.

But mothers thus distracted are off track
The dangers all increase when boys come back.

1 Nephi 5: 8

And when she saw the boys make safe return
And held them tightly in her anxious arms
She saw the miracle of God's concern.
And changed her tune from murmurings to charms.

Her language now is full of surety
No longer does her glass of life look spilled
She speaks as one who has complete security
That every glass before her is well filled.

She sounds a lot like how young Nephi talked
When he was first commanded; "Go and do"
Back then, we know, she rather clearly balked
But now she's made a change from that debut.

It's possible to join God's labour force
At any time (before the end), of course.

1 Nephi 5: 9

I think I understand the metaphor
That sacrificial animals transmit
But thinking of this blood and fire and gore
Offends my sensibilities a bit.

It would not be an easy way for me
To celebrate the saving of my kin
I would not find in it the slightest glee
To draw a knife across some critter's chin.

And roasting animals I've barely killed
To watch the smoke go upward as a sign
Of thanks to heaven for a prayer fulfilled
Is not the way I worship the divine.

Yet almost every homecoming I do
Ends up with something done as barbeque.

1 Nephi 5: 10

Sometimes our gratitude seems quite enough
We put the gift aside and never delve
Into the actual reading of the stuff
Quite often books we get we simply shelve.

Or we might take a token look at it
To understand its message or its trend
But often other duties won't permit
A study from the start right to the end.

And truthfully no one could read them all
There's more to life than reading all the time
So since your piece of bookish pie's so small
Confine your appetite to those most prime.

This gift that Lehi got, on plates of brass
Is one a lot of folks will just let pass.

1 Nephi 5: 11

We study in the sky the stars and such
And look at fossils and at rocks and bones
And hope to understand from this so much
Of ancient and mysterious unknowns.

We poke around in oceans and in seas
Investigate volcanoes and earthquakes
We do our carbon dating on old trees
And study lizards, dinosaurs and snakes.

We even learn some legends and folk tales
And myths of Greeks, Etruscans and the like
And marvel at the size of great white whales
And wonder at a random lightening strike.

But when you seek the origin of man
It's best to read about it if you can.

1 Nephi 5: 12

If all your past is just a mystery
They say you are condemned to do again
Those things you didn't know from history
And suffer needlessly repeated pain.

And so a record of mistakes by anyone
Is just the thing to stop that awful skid
Of doing once again what once was done
Avoiding for yourself what others did.

And heaven knows the Jews have had their share
Of troubles brought about by sin and woe
And so a record of their long despair
Is just the thing we really ought to know.

Besides, along with stories of their grief
Are listed all the blessings of belief.

1 Nephi 5: 13

Imagine Lehi in his desert tent
Alone at last with precious brassy plates
Aware that what he had was heaven sent
In awe of how each holy word translates.

Excitement must have charged his very soul
And made it difficult to concentrate
And fighting for emotional control
He read. While others, outside, had to wait.

A prophet reading prophets from the start
A seer now seeing what was in God's heart
A revelator reveling in his art
A choice and chosen vessel set apart.

And meanwhile, outside, in the desert sand
A family anxious for the next command.

1 Nephi 5: 14

How many of us have a famous past
Some ancestor who did himself so proud
That what he did is yet quite unsurpassed
His profile high above the normal crowd.

And if we know about that special guy
Who lives in legend, yet is still our kin
Does that in any sense or way imply
Some bit of our own specialness within.

And aren't we all just brothers from the start
The children of one father of us all
So what's the point of setting some apart
Of bragging of connections who stood tall.

I wonder if what matters is to love
And learn from them, not just to be proud of.

1 Nephi 5: 15

You've got to see the parallel that's here
Between the Israelites who left the Nile
And these that left Jerusalem in fear
And how their God was with them all the while.

This study of captivity and sin
Of how the Lord preserves his chosen ones
Has patterns also that are quite akin
To Adam, Abraham and all their sons.

And Babylon or Egypt or L.A.
Or Salem or Las Vegas or N'Orleans
Each point to ancient and to latter day
Captivity and preservation scenes.

So study all these patterns and rejoice
In how God rescues those who heed his voice.

1 Nephi 5: 16

These days it seems some maiden aunt or such
Is likely to be keeping family news
And not the dilettante who's out of touch
The guy who's over friendly with the booze.

But maybe there was more prestige back then
In making genealogies a daily must
Perhaps it was a badge of power when
You held the secrets of the family trust.

It seems our Lehi was himself surprised
To learn the branches of his family tree
It's clear he hadn't got himself apprized
Of from which tribe the family came to be.

So even back then there were those, alas
Who fail to take the family history class.

1 Nephi 5: 17

This Lehi had a thing with reading writ
The sacred kind, at least, or so we've heard
It filled him with the Spirit, every whit
And showed him things which yet had not
occurred.

So more than just the info that he found
The scriptures were a catalytic feast
They changed his very nature all around
A man becoming prophet and high priest.

And well we might try something near the same
By taking of the word of God within
We could be changed, inspired to proclaim
The sacred things in store for all our kin.

But many never risk a prophet's call
Their scripture study effort's far too small.

1 Nephi 5: 18

I'm sitting in the sand beside our tent
The flies that follow camels buzzing round
And in my purse, not even one red cent
And no idea where this bunch is bound.

And fear that someone's out to get us too
Is not just paranoia, this is real
Cause we'd be in a pickle and a stew
If someone saw the smoke from our last meal.

And here in all this hopelessness and pain
My father babbles on about his seed
His rantings are unhinged and so insane
That logic or debate gets little heed.

The surest way to save these plates, I say
Is bury them deep in the sand today.

1 Nephi 5: 19

I don't think brass will rust or waste away
At least not for a great long time I'd guess
But who am I to speculate this way
I'm weak at metallurgy I confess.

But what will not be dimmed, I understand
Is something more important than mere plates
It more about the words etched in by hand
The "prophesy" and not the brassy traits.

As Lehi held these plates that held the word
His vision was expanded and explained
And just as sure as prophesy occurred
The prophet had detractors who complained.

The secret seems to be to learn to cherish
These sacred things that truly never perish.

1 Nephi 5: 20

He didn't say they'd strived or done their best
He didn't say they'd just made an attempt
He didn't say they'd made a stab or quest
He never claimed or asked to be exempt.

He didn't speak of effort or of sweat
He didn't say they made a valiant try
He didn't give excuses or regret
And never did he waiver or deny.

He didn't even say how hard it was
Or hint of deeds of sacrifice untold
He didn't seem to hesitate or pause
To say they went and did as they were told.

How many of us also will prove true
To that great saying "I will go and do"?

1 Nephi 5: 21

Opinions were divided in this clan
About the value of preserving writ
While Nephi was an unabashed fan
Two brothers weren't, and that's what caused
the split.

The Lord may make an errand for a son
A task, a test, a trial, so it seems
But in the end the fruits of what's been done
May not accord with every child's dreams.

Yet each had risked his life to gather these
And lost great family treasures left unsold
And now the outcome seemed to only please
The ones who valued scripture more than gold.

Though Laman, at the time, decried the need
I hope, by now, he sees it for his seed.

1 Nephi 5: 22

Consider packing up for any trip
Of sorting precious stuff from out the junk
And choosing just with what we will equip
Our wagon or our suitcase or our trunk.

There's always on our list some things we "must"
And other things fall into "mights" or "wants"
Still others on a flimsy whim we trust
Will come in handy at some future haunts.

They used to say, as wisdom for the road
To take just half the clothes you think you'll need
And twice the cash you probably planned to
load
If you expect your traveling to succeed.

But here's a tip that's from the Lord and wise:
To always pack the Word with your supplies.

1 Nephi Chapter 6

Sometimes a thing is written to amuse
Or shock, or teach or only entertain
Some writers want to simply cry the blues
While others have in mind financial gain.

Some never do explain just why they wrote
And truth to tell their purposes confuse
And some write books where better just a note
Would satisfy to explicate their views.

But Nephi didn't leave the slightest doubt
That his intent was that men be enticed
And so he tells us that this book's about
Persuading men to come to Jesus Christ.

Not meant to please in worldly ways, these plates,
Engravings which the gift of God translates.

1 Nephi Chapter 7

Tradition is that youngest sons don't preach
To disobedient brothers in the clan
Reproving elders should be out of reach
A babe, it seems, should not correct a man.

And almost all we hear about who fail
To keep this simple rule of etiquette
At least the way the scripture stories tell
Have troubles that they cannot soon forget.

And thus with Nephi as with Jacob's Joe
We find attempted murder is no jest
It's mighty dangerous for little bro
To be the one God sets above the rest.

I wonder if these younger prophets thought
"Why wasn't I the first my dad begot?"

1 Nephi 8: 1

Beyond the wall of water, seeds not vines,
They gathered, carried, spread. Two nation's
fruits
And grains to be together intertwined
To ever after share entangled roots.

And far more, even than the DNA
Great promise followed every seed they chose
While farming in forbidding distant clay
Was all that they were thinking, we suppose.

Yet here this introduction to a dream
Of sweetest fruit of any tree of all
Foreshadowed by these seeds the holy theme
Of overcoming what we call "the fall".

To plant with faith in distant promised land
What seeds will any dreamer need on hand?

1 Nephi 8: 2

"Behold, I've dreamed a dream, or as we say
I've seen a vision." Lehi said to them
By now, one has to know how that would play
With sons he might have nicknamed La' and
Lem.

What thoughts of errands, chastisement or such
Must then have flooded into each boy's head
To whiners who had heard his dreams too much
Announcements of a vision. Then came dread.

One thing you could not say of father Le'
That he refused to give out awful news
This dream, the worst of any that could be
Was not the sort that tender parents choose.

But maybe, like his sons, old father L
Misunderstood, at first, what he would tell.

1 Nephi 8: 3

I don't suppose that Lehi's dream surprised
This patriarch a bit about his boys
He must have previously realized
Just which would give him reason to rejoice.

But still to learn that any child's on course
And of their seed, great many will be saved
Is something that's a sure and welcome source
Of joy, to all who parenting have braved.

And yet, if only some are headed right
No parent can be happy to his core
The offspring who don't lean toward the light
Are bound to weigh upon a parent more.

Perhaps it's kinder not to know for sure
Just which, if any, children will endure.

1 Nephi 8: 4

I know too much of dark and dreary places
Of wilderness and being far from home
Since nothing but accusatory faces
Have greeted me since we began to roam.

At least I have my brother Lemuel
One kindred in amongst my hostile kin
Unlike my brothers Sam (not Samuel)
And Nephi, (who might be my father's twin).

Old Lem's the sort of friend who doesn't judge
Or wag a wicked finger in my way
He never gripes, or whines or holds a grudge
But goes along with anything I say.

Old man! Your fears are such a bunch of lies!
Your dreams, excuses just to criticize.

1 Nephi Chapter 9

Some people won't do much unless they know
The purpose for each rule or each command
They grumble if they're asked to come or go
Without full explanations right on hand.

Each time they want to judge if what they're
asked
Is worth the effort that they'll have to make
They weigh the value of each law or task
To see if it's a chance they choose to take.

Some others just use faith to make their choice
Deciding to submit and to obey
Relying once and always on the Voice
Then holding to that plan in everyway.

It seems that it was often Nephi's lot
To deal with plates for reasons he knew not.

1 Nephi Chapter 10

We get our news hot off the press these days
Or watch it on TV on CNN
And suffer few restrictions or delays
As it gets played and then replayed again.

Within the hour we hear if bombs are dropped
We're told when airplanes crash how many die
And if a flood is started or gets stopped
We're sure to hear about the how and why.

Yes now the standard of reporting's high
It has become an all important trade
But still, it only deals with things gone by
Neglecting all the news yet to be made.

I'd like to hear predictions he might bring
If Lehi was a guest on Larry King.

1 Nephi 11: 1

Some interviews are long and drawn out
And barely seem to get to what counts most
And leave us in unease or even doubt
About what was intended by our host.

Not so the queries of this Spirit friend
Who came to Nephi as he pondered deep
And sought to bring to light this simple end;
What sorts of wishes did young Nephi keep?

So if your quest's designed to find the heart
And learn the soul of someone as a test
It would be well to emulate this art
To find, quite simply, what they want the best.

Begin by boldly asking their desires
The answer should tell all the test requires.

1 Nephi 11: 3

No greater joy can any father know
Than that his chi-ld walks in wisdom's way
And for that child to learn the way to go
He has to want, to ask, to plead, to pray.

The marvel and the wonder calmly sings
Although unheard, an echo, certain, keen
In every sober child's breast of things
That fathers, gone before have truly seen.

And all that's needed to unlock the song
And open up the view that ages knew
Is for the child to ask, to yearn, to long,
The blessings of the fathers to renew.

But what of sons of fathers blind to love
What calls their hearts to seek for things
above?

1 Nephi Chapter 12

The angel said, "Behold the promised land!"
He looked and saw his seed. Now multitude.
As many as an ocean's grains of sand
Descendants of a nasty family feud.

And slaughter, wars and battles held his eyes
As cities sank and rocks and mountains fell
And lightening filled the anxious troubled skies
While fires burned and turned the earth to hell.

And then he saw the Lamb descend and peace
And faith and righteous judgment filled the land
And all unholy tumult seemed to cease
As worthy oneness made a mighty stand.

Yet soon the scene went back to blood and war
Dark shadows warning what this book is for.

1 Nephi Chapter 13

Most men don't bother much with what's gone on
And even less do we consider well
The forecasts that transcend tomorrow's dawn
We're focussed in the moment where we dwell.

Oh sure, if angels gave us guided tours
Of past and future happenings of note
We'd pay attention to times distant shores
At least the ones we felt weren't too remote.

But paying heed to some third party claim
Of visionary glimpses by the way
Is even less the spark that lights the flame
To heat up honest passions in our day.

Yet some will read of visions Nephi braved
And learn thereby, we hope, how men are saved.

1 Nephi Chapter 14

This chapter drives me crazy I'll admit
So lucid and insightful... oh so clear!
Describing how the Lamb and Gentile fit
Into God's plan for Israel far and near.

Apostasy and restoration themes
And promises for those who do repent
Exposure of abominable schemes
And where the devil's children will be sent!

But just as Nephi gets to where we are
To things we want to know the most of all
He tells us of a publication bar
And says the rest's the Revelator's call.

I like the book of Revelation too
But find it _so_ much harder to construe!

1 Nephi 14:7

Three things that bother almost everyone:
Behavior that is less than their desire
Repeated over time and over done
Strong habits that deny a life that's higher.

The second thing is blindness to our faults
Missteps we see in others we reprove
Though gladly practiced in our daily waltz
Hypocrisy's built in to every move.

Add to these two; destruction as a friend
We invite ruin like it was our pal
Destroying ourselves and others in the end
The fatal flaw of every guy and gal.

Addiction, blindness and destruction... When?
We get them every time we stoop to sin.

1 Nephi 15:1

Suppose the Spirit carried you away
And showed you things you couldn't hardly tell
And showered you with wisdom's perfect ray
And put you under heaven's faultless spell.

Suppose that even questions never posed
Were answered by the Spirit as you dreamed
And nothing to your heart was undisclosed
And nothing sacred to you unredeemed.

And then, when all this spiritual affair
Had passed, and life was "everyday" again
Where would you go, the first of all, to share
To testify, to marvel, to explain?

It seems, when youthful prophet's dreams are spent
You'll find them straightway back in father's tent.

1 Nephi 15:2

Ah, peaceful home. The sanctuary place.
Where weary, troubled, family members meet
To find respite, and rest a teary face
And from a hostile wor-ld make retreat.

And where your news of triumph or defeat
Your joyful glories and your solemn griefs
Are met with strains of praise or solace sweet
And no one thinks to challenge your beliefs.

And while, at times, each one of us may feel
Our home is thusly organized to share
Yet knowing such a home is an ideal
We mourn because, for constancy, it's rare.

Disputing in the home is such a curse
It's hard to think of anything that's worse.

1 Nephi 15: 3

What child cannot seem to understand
A portion, sometimes great, of what is giv'n
By parents as a warning or command?
The one who, for the knowledge, has not striv'n.

What person will not hold to what is true
Or feel the pow'r of learning to obey
And seems unsure of things he one time knew?
The one whose heart is far too hard to pray.

What pilgrim will not look to where he goes
Or focus on the light of worthy thought
And fails to keep to pathways that he knows?
The one who will not get to where he ought.

If I could bless myself with one desire
It might be that I'm willing to inquire.

1 Nephi 15:4

Two veils protect the average Joe from woe
The first that makes premortal life a blur
And one which makes it so that we don't know
Details of things before that they occur.

So men without the prophet's curse are free
From grief about what hasn't happened yet
They have few worries about things to be
And only suffer "past" and "now" regret.

It's quite a burden to add future stress
To worries and to losses we all share
So seeric power doesn't only bless
It adds a heavy load of extra care.

When Nephi prayed to learn a little more
He got a lot more than he bargained for.

1 Nephi 15:5

Another fella's troubles might be great
He might be overcome with pain and loss
His misery so steep it's past debate
His spirit broken by his heavy cross.

And someone might be poor or left alone
Or frightened or discouraged or oppressed
And others might be hungry, lame, or prone
To fail at almost each and every test.

And yet, it seems, no matter how depressed
That someone else can be as time goes by
That fella's almost certainly well blessed
Compared to what afflictions fall on me!

There's nothing quite so proximate and real
As grief and pain and sorrow that *I* feel.

1 Nephi 15:6

There is no comfort for the righteous man
But to begin to minister again
To offer of yourself must be the plan
Or be consumed by misery and pain.

Delivering the word may not save each
Who hears an anxious brother's warning voice
His agency restricts your actual reach
As learning is the hearer's solemn choice.

But always blest is he who speaks the word
Whose call to turn from sin is strong and sure
No matter, for himself, if spurned or heard
The process is his private peaceful cure.

So even as you mourn the rebel's fate
Rise up! Speak out! And make your grief abate.

1 Nephi 15: 7

Some details Lehi must have failed to share
And bits of allegory were unclear
But still, the brothers knew it meant; Beware!
And that it promised consequence severe.

The bits about the branches of the tree
And how the Gentile nations figured in
Were lessons that the brothers could not see
And seemed to chaff their permanent thin skin.

So what they did was argue and dispute
As if by bickering they could win out
They mocked the solemn need to gather fruit
And proved the dream was right about their doubt.

It seems when things are difficult to know
Disputing might not be the way to go.

1 Nephi 15:8

When final judgment comes upon us each
A single question, serious and true
May be enough to clear, or to impeach,
To settle with an effortless review.

This query may seem innocent, facile,
Not having searching depth or lasting goal
And be dismissed by those with hearts of guile
As foolish irksome meaningless control.

But think. The answer, if it be as right
As prayer, and flowing with the force of faith
What glory by its magnifying light
A worthy, perfect, affirmation saith.

"Have ye inquired of the Lord?" He asked
And every cunning pretext was unmasked.

1 Nephi 15:9

Behold the lie in every sinning heart
Pathetic cry of those who will not try
To knock, to seek, to ask the better part
Because they say that heaven won't reply.

It seems too nice, too neat, too fine, too thin
To hold as even reasoning or thought
No logic tells them there's no answer when
They first deny, before it's even sought.

Beware this baseless, spineless, pale excuse
Whenever you're enticed by Satan's voice
Do not exploit this logical abuse
The lie that says you really have no choice.

I would not want to murmur in this way
Then have to live with what the Lord would say.

1 Nephi 15:10

That line between disciple and dissent
A barrier of stony opaque thought
As easy penetrated as cement
Will lend itself to discourse overwrought.

"Why don't you get it?" followers will wail,
Across that wall, a cry to those who doubt,
And from the other side they never fail
To raise their scornful answer with a shout.

You cannot linger on that line and muse
Between the factions firm on either side
The dissidence demands you quickly choose
Your place, on left, or right, of the divide.

However nothing says you cannot change
And so, I guess, that's why the strong exchange.

1 Nephi 15:11

We turn as on a wheel from here to there
Then back to here again, resolved, redeemed,
Safe harboured once again in heaven's care
Life's journey's like a lesson that we've dreamed.

It's all, I've heard, just one eternal round
Although we like the notion that we grow
There is a sense, that nothing's newly found
It's all pursuit of what we used to know.

Remember, if you can, and you'll receive,
Forget, and all that matters is denied
It's only when you've proved that you believe
That you'll remember where the answers hide.

And purest powers of memory reveal -
There is no past, nor future, on this wheel.

1 Nephi 15:12

Be broken, busted, out of order too
Kaput, not working, wrecked and broken down
Be pureed, mashed and crumbled in a stew
Be tattered like a tired paper crown.

Cut off, or severed, lopped or sliced or slashed
Be amputated, orphaned, disengaged
Be pruned, be trimmed, incised or meanly gashed
Be lonely, lost, abandoned or upstaged.

Be separated from your kin and place
Be all of that, and less, and yet in fact
You have a heritage you can't erase
Your house, though distant, still remains intact.

I am a child of God the children sing
Estranged perhaps, but still a future king.

1 Nephi 15:13

I wonder about DNA and such
If blood lines figure in the scheme of things
If being French, Arabian or Dutch
Will matter when we meet our King of Kings?

Is being Jewish something to desire
Or Gentileness a detriment to fate
How can a certain lineage make Him smile
While other houses get the sign to "wait"?

I'm sure it isn't really about race
Or legacy, or lineage or descent
For though I know that houses have their place
No privilege through pedigree is meant.

Yet history and prophesy prescribe
That each of belongs within a tribe.

1 Nephi 15:14

If you were one, not careful with your gift
Who did not share or teach your children well
Who chose, instead, to let the devil sift
Your soul wrapped up in bitter chains of hell.

You have stood by for generations now
And likely seen the mis'ry that you caused
And probably, despaired of if, and how
This avalanche of evil could be paused.

Still, prophets promised that before the end
The points of saving doctrine would be taught
So everyone could find and comprehend
The covenant by which their souls were bought.

You'd wish this happy promise would come swift
If you were one, not careful with your gift.

1 Nephi 15: 15

Who is your rock? Where do you go for strength?
And when you gather what's it like, your fold?
Who gets your praises when you praise at length
Your plaudits when you make a tribute bold?

And when your soul is hungered and grows weak
Where do you look for nourishment and aid?
For comfort and relief when things go bleak?
Where have you really turned when you have
prayed?

A fateful day will come when you'll admit
That all those worldly places were a waste
That nothing saves until you will submit
Until your confidence is better placed.

Why not rejoice right now and give God praise?
Why wait until that fateful day of days?

1 Nephi 15: 16

There must be reason for these lengthy times
When no one has the light to find the course
Perhaps to magnify apostate crimes
And emphasize the depth of evil's force.

Were these divine divisions prearranged
To come and go beneath uncertain light
So many born and buried still estranged
Not even comprehending their own plight?

Predicting separation from their roots
And that a grafting time would come some day
May presuppose a rift that heaven suits
Though why it might I really couldn't say.

Still, in the end, remembrance will prevail
And we're assured that Israel cannot fail.

1 Nephi 15:16 (#2)

Displaced, dislodged, dismembered, set apart
But still no less an olive than the tree
An olive branch, still olive in its heart
Since what it was, is what it yet will be.

Forgotten, lost, forsaken, left alone
Across the trackless sea, a lonesome land
Like vineyards hid by awesome walls of stone
Or cities buried under years of sand.

Two times uncovered by the God of love
The land and people first and then the bough
Exposed from both below and up above
The times and places such as He'd allow.

And from this dust two seeds of growth explode
An olive branch and leaves of purest gold!

1 Nephi 15: 17

The best and worst of all creation here
Assembled to enact the greatest play
No game, nor chance, attach this mortal sphere
This earth, this life, this crucible, this way.

Beyond unbounded, infinite and more
The pow'rs that clashed hereon had to be set
So that the test would certainly ensure
No doubt, no shrinking, dodging or regret.

And so the very people of the King
His kin, his house, his family, his tribe
Would have to be the ones to help to bring
This awful sacrifice for silvered bribe.

Small thing to scatter those who did this deed
Great thing to save them in their hour of need.

1 Nephi 15:18

Seed scattered, gathered, scattered, sown and
grown
Across the earth, across the endless years
Seed gathered, scattered, gathered, overblown
All pointing to a covenant of tears.

Oh father Abraham! Your children weep
And brawl among themselves in fierce delight
They sow, they tend, they cultivate and reap
A harvest of despair, and death, and spite.

The promise is that out of all this ire
Will come some hope, some love, some rest,
someday
Not just some great apocalyptic fire
That's set to burn impurities away.

And all, at last, as kindred will be blessed
And lie, we hope, on Father Abram's breast.

1 Nephi 15:19

The wisdom of a prophet to an ear
Belonging not to one who loves the word
And not attuned to comprehend or hear
Will pass as though it wasn't even heard.

Why bother preaching to that hardened soul
Who lets you know he's heard it all before
Who will not entertain the story's whole
As if his solemn duty's to ignore?

I guess we never really ever know
When testimony may impact a man
Or when a bit of knowledge we bestow
Will change his understanding of the plan.

But if my brothers' hearing was that slow
I might have left off preaching long ago.

1 Nephi 15:20

We like to have our villains well defined
Our heroes plainly listed just as well
We sort the good and bad of all mankind
Into the "wicked weasels" and the "swell".

And heading up the designated class
Of evil types in father Lehi's tent
Were Lemuel and Laman, unsurpassed
For wickedness and mischievous intent.

Yet Nephi's many words, this time, were heard
And humbled hardened hearts grew soft, for now,
As angry brothers finally were spurred
To listen to the doctrines that endow.

Persuasive, patient teaching pacified
And brothers, for a time, reclassified.

1 Nephi 15: 21

When Lehi dreamed of iron rods and mist
Of darkness clouding strait and narrow path
And people needing badly to resist
A multitude of scorning mocking wrath.

He recognized his children in his dream
Some boldly holding to the iron rod
And others with the scorners 'cross the stream,
Divided in their will to follow God.

He must have been delighted, later on,
When finally the ones he dreamed were lost
Did question what conclusions should be drawn.
What parting from the tree of life might cost?

What do they mean, the things my father saw?
The wisdom of the question fills with awe.

1 Nephi 15:22

Why does a tree so ably stand for this?
The taking up of water, earth and air
And by the course of photosynthesis
A sweet and wholesome fruit the tree will bear.

What other process mirrors the tree in this?
The taking up of water, earth and air
And by His gift the Sun of Righteousness
A sweet and wholesome fruit will also share.

How do we benefit from all of this?
The taking up of water, earth and air
And by our living feast upon, in bliss,
A sweet and wholesome fruit beyond compare.

And where and when will all of this be done?
When, like that tree, we turn towards the sun.

1 Nephi 15:23

I might be going soon to France or Spain
I'm free, quite free, to wander where I will
To climb a mountain, run across a plain,
Or visit China, Thailand or Brazil.

I could be planning something in the north
Or days of leisure on a desert isle
I could stay home, or travel back and forth
Upon the Themes, the Amazon, or Nile.

I need no compass, chart or lighthouse ray
To tell me where to go, or when, or how
It's up to me to choose to go or stay
To travel later on or here and now.

But if I want to journey back to God
I need to find and hold the iron rod.

1 Nephi 15:24

I think it's prob'bly not the flaming parts
That make a pilgrim's eyes lose sight. You'll find
Instead it's likely that with fiery darts
The adversary's sending smoke to blind.

And everyone's affected, more or less
And anyone can perish, in an hour
Unless he keeps his bearings in the press
The acrid bitter mists will overpow'r.

Escape will only come to those who hear
The words the Father sends to us in love
We're lost unless we hold them fast and dear
Our eyes too veiled to see the prize above.

So hear and hearken, heed, and hold the rod
And fight your way determinedly to God.

1 Nephi 15:25

It seems, sometimes, we weaken and obey
Despite our knowing that we're always wronged
Our brother's energy has such a sway
His potent protestations so prolonged.

And thus, from time to time, as he exhorts
We lose our confidence and take the bait
And wearied of our normal brave retorts
We play his silly game without debate.

And yet, no doubt, as circumstances change
And he moves on to worry other prey
We'll notice that his arguments were strange
And reaffirm submission's not our way.

So asking harmless questions is no threat
When, after all, we're sure we'll soon forget.

1 Nephi 15:26

When father dreams his dreams he's quick to tell
The scenes he sees in visionary ways
And yet, it seems, it takes another spell
To get some meaning out of all this haze.

And once before he wish'd I'd be a stream
A river flowing into righteousness
Another crazy allegory theme
Just one more mixed up metaphor, I'd guess.

A river could mean anything! Come on!
I'll ask, but don't be fooled, I do not care
You know that my conclusions are foregone
But go ahead, I'm asking, now, please share.

What is this river business all about?
Give me your benefit. I'll add the doubt.

1 Nephi 15: 27

We never get it right, well, not at first
The scene around is more than we can bear
Our witness unavoidably is cursed
No two accounts will ever quite compare.

This overload, predictable, and known
Makes fodder for the scoffer, mean and cold
Who says since inconsistencies are shown
We can't rely on anything that's told.

And so the law, of witnesses, abused
Allows the cunning doubter to deceive
And leaves some earnest questioners confused
A bold attack on those who would believe.

What's really, line on line, precepts to choose
The scorners tend to call, conflicting views.

1 Nephi 15:28

Along each briny ocean beach and shore
There's straits and inlets, seas and sounds and
bays
And also, everywhere, there's gulfs galore
They're quite the widespread geographic craze.

The Gulf of Mexico is one we know
The Gulf of Bothnia a rarer brand
And ev'ry map will almost surely show
A Gulf in Aden, Oman, and Thailand.

The Persian Gulf, just now, is really strong
The Gulf of Guinea never had a voice
But there's no greater gulf in word or song
Than that which comes from exercise of choice.

Between the saints of God and wicked ends:
The awful Gulf of Misery, my friends.

1 Nephi 15:29

To those who favor sin as what to do
Who murder, steal and make a lie for fun
Who make a friend of anything untrue
It's nice they'll have a home when they get
done.

To those who like destruction and distress
Who hate and fight and hold a grudge for sport
Who never met a law they don't transgress
It's nice they'll have there own "Club Med" resort.

To those who are unfaithful, rude and proud
Who take advantage, cheat, and love deceit
Whose speech is grumbly, murmuring, yet loud
It's nice they'll get their very own retreat.

It's nice they'll have a place where they can
dwell
Too bad it has to be that awful hell.

1 Nephi 15:30 (with reference to Matthew 25)

The Son of Man shall sit upon his throne
And gather every nation, tribe and man
Before Him, to divide into his zone
Some right, some left, according to the plan.

And on the right, we know, he puts the sheep
Because they've learned to serve with care and love
And on the left, we see, the goats will weep
And feign surprise at judgments from above.

Between the sheep and goats, a great divide
No simple fence of stone, or wood, or wire
Instead a grand partition, high and wide
Impassable and bright like flaming fire.

It's justice, from their God, won't let them blend
Dividing good from evil in the end.

1 Nephi 15: 31

We wander down the paths of life unsure
If what we feel and see is really real
And even more so when we end this tour
We question if the next is mere "ideal".

The spiritual and temporal oppose
Two wholly diff'rent spheres we like to say
Dichotomies so clear, as we suppose
That everyone agrees things are that way.

Yet science cannot prove the soul exists
Nor do its subatomic forays show
That matter's any more than an abyss
A solemn void of emptiness and woe.

I guess it's not surprising, as we've found,
Distinctions without difference abound

1 Nephi 15:32

To earn their way until their days are spent
Some people swing an ax or shake a saw
While others toil with words and argument
Or work the healing arts or crafts or law

Some barely make enough to stay alive
Some bear and raise up children for their job
Some work at being sick, while others thrive
Some beg, some hunt, some barter and some rob.

Yet whether with his back and sweat and brawn
Or by the force of mind and cunning art
The work a man performs will someday spawn
The means of final judgment of his heart.

I'd like to know, along the way, somehow
What's coming then, from what I'm doing now.

1 Nephi 15:33

Here on the earth there is no place quite clean
To some degree it's dirty everywhere
There filthy, fresh, and lots that's in between
Perfection eludes water, land and air.

In heaven there's a faultlessness severe
There is no dust, nor lint, nor thing unclean
No filth permitted, far or wide or near
The place is pure, all perfect and pristine.

And so a place was made for those of us
Who could not measure up to heaven's norm
A place where sloppy, dingy, filthy Gus
Could evermore feel comfy, snug and warm.

It takes great faith, to spotlessness aspire
When all our lives we've wallowed in this mire.

1 Nephi 15: 34

All wise and loving parents make a place
For every child in their tender care
No one's excluded from the father's grace
Or left without a caring mother's share.

And yet, of course, all children have their way
And some will turn from parents, God, and man
And shout their right to call the night a day
Yet ev'n for these we trust there is a plan.

Some place designed for those who merit less
Who trade away for pottage what is great
A place where love and kindness ever bless
Each child in his undeserving state.

And privileges will vary, child to child
And separate the worthy from the wild.

1 Nephi 15:35

The wise man knows he can't do all jobs well
And so some things he doesn't try to do
So when it came to building awful hell
God let the contract out to one who knew.

The devil won the contract fair and square
To make a place where those who hated good
Would feel a proper measure of despair
A bleak and mean and hopeless
neighbourhood.

I'd have to guess the craftsmanship was true
To Satan's need to lie and steal and cheat
And so the final product is a stew
Of false and flimsy, faithless, and deceit.

And now the job's done right in every way
For every wretch, a wretched place to stay.

1 Nephi 15:36

The multitudes who feel their way to hell
And crowd the road of scorn and ridicule
Have made a lasting choice of where they'll
dwell
A choice defined by such a simple rule.

We either seek the tree of life - and bear
The shame of earthly mockery - or hold
The iron rod of heaven's will - and share
That gift, most precious gift of God - not gold.

Rejected are the wicked from the tree
And from those righteous harvesting its fruit
Not barred or banned or proscribed, they are
free
It's just that they have chosen this pursuit.

The pity is for those, I guess, who think
That they would backslide only to the brink.

About the Poet

Tom Matkin was born and raised in Cardston, Alberta. He served a mission in France and learned the law in Edmonton where he met his wife Betty. After Law School they lived in Calgary for a year and then moved to Cardston in 1975 to open a law office and they haven't budged since. For many years Tom has read through the Book of Mormon every month, and just for fun and to forestall the valid criticism that this practice discourages a close understanding of the text he writes these little sonnets. Writing and reading poetry in a rigid form such as the sonnet is an amazing way to discover hidden treasures in language and thought and it is Tom's hope that you find a few treasures here for yourself.

Note from the author

This isn't the sort of project that anyone could finish in a lifetime although I have written many more sonnets and poems than appear here. But publishing what I've done so far on the first 15 chapters of 1 Nephi seemed to be a reasonable place to draw a line and publish, so I did. Maybe more volumes will follow at a later date.

Postscript

Fifty Reasons Not to Write Poems

Misunderstood, ignored, confused and mocked
Perplexed, bemused, belittled, overwrought
Surprised, mistaken, lost and mildly shocked
Dismissed, dismayed, displeased, dissuade, distraught.

Exposed, at risk, alone, unsafe, quite bare
Critique, breakdown, analysis, review
Uncalled, unjust, unwarranted, unfair
Depressed, discouraged, taunted, all askew.

Rebuffed, forgot, denied, gainsaid, left out
Befuddled mystified and bamboozled
A sulk, a wink, a nod, a silly pout
Cajoled, consoled, untold, it all gets old.

Still, there are other reasons by the score
Most people don't write poems anymore.

Made in the USA
Charleston, SC
25 October 2015